THE Perfect Pumpkin

GAIL DAMEROW

A Storey Publishing Book

Storey Communications, Inc.
Schoolhouse Road
Pownal, Vermont 05261

The mission of Storey Communications is to serve our customers
by publishing practical information that encourages personal independence
in harmony with the environment.

Edited by Gwen Steege and Deborah Burns
Cover and text design by Cindy McFarland
Cover photographs by Gary Hall (front) and W. Atlee Burpee (back)
Text production by Susan Bernier and Erin Lincourt
Line drawings by Susan Berry Langsten
Indexed by Susan Olason, Indexes & Knowledge Maps

Printed in the United States by R.R. Donnelley & Sons
10 9 8 7 6 5 4 3 2 1

Library of Congress Cataloging-in-Publication Data

Damerow, Gail.
    The perfect pumpkin / Gail Damerow.
        p.   cm.
    "A Storey Publishing Book"
    Includes bibliographical references and index.
    ISBN 0-88266-993-1 (pb : alk. paper)
    1. Pumpkin.   2. Pumpkin—Utilization.   3. Cookery (Pumpkin).   I. Title.
SB347.D36   1997
635'.62—dc21   97-12562
                                                      CIP

Contents

Acknowledgments

Heartfelt thanks to everyone who helped gather information for this book, then waited patiently for its arrival, especially: Brent Loy of University of New Hampshire for information on naked seed varieties; Wayne Hackney of New Milford, Connecticut, for details on growing giant pumpkins; Robert J. Rouse of University of Maryland for data on pumpkin pests and diseases; my mother Dixie, chief recipe tester, and husband Allan, chief pumpkin eater; and all those who contributed delicious recipes. My special thanks go to heirloom seed saver Glenn Drowns of Calamus, Iowa, and to the king of giant pumpkins Howard Dill and his son Danny of Windsor, Nova Scotia, for reading my manuscript and helping fill in the gaps pertaining to their respective areas of expertise.

— Gail Damerow

Introducing the Versatile Pumpkin

If you grow pumpkins, you will be happy when you pick them. Savor what you feel, in addition to what you taste. Enjoy the blossoms — if pumpkins were rare, gardeners would pamper them in greenhouses just for their extraordinary flowers.

— J. L. Hudson, Seedsman
Redwood City, California, 1995

WHEN SOMEONE MENTIONS PUMPKINS, you probably think of jagged-toothed jack-o'-lanterns or Thanksgiving pies. But versatile pumpkins have far more to offer than these traditional uses. Even before a pumpkin forms, the vine's tender young leaves can become tasty steamed or boiled greens, and the edible blossoms make an attractive garnish or a delicious stuffed-and-fried side dish. The immature fruits add a pleasant crunch to salads or stir-fries, mature pumpkins yield both multipurpose meat and nutritious seeds, and the cheerful orange shells are easily hollowed out to make containers that double as serving bowls or cooking pots.

Besides their many culinary offerings, pumpkins are indispensable mood setters for autumn festivities. And they have become objects of intense competition: Who can grow the biggest pumpkin, who can carve

1

the most imaginative jack-o'-lantern, who can throw one the farthest? And when all else is said and done, pumpkins are relished as a time-honored winter feed by goats, cattle, pigs, and poultry.

Pumpkins have something to offer the dedicated enthusiast year-round: spring planting, summer cultivation, fall fun, winter storage. Adding further to its appeal, this best-known member of the squash family comes in a multitude of varieties, with shells ranging in color from orange to yellow, white, green, and even blue; flesh ranging in texture from mealy to meaty; and sizes ranging from gourmet miniatures that nestle in the palm of your hand to mammoth record setters big enough to carve into a child's playhouse.

Besides all this, pumpkins are incredibly easy to raise. The lush, fast-growing, prolific vine is an ideal first-garden confidence builder for a child or novice adult. But even if you're an expert, there's something decidedly magical about spotting those glowing orange globes peeping out from a sea of sprawling green vines.

In short, pumpkins speak to our elemental need to reap abundance from the land. No wonder people of all ages are intrigued by the pumpkin.

–1–
The Great American Pumpkin

Pumpkins are an American call to irrationality and excess, a tribute to the bounty of our hemisphere.

— Linden Staciokas
Harrowsmith Country Life, 1993

UNKNOWN IN EUROPE BEFORE the time of Columbus, the pumpkin is unique to the Americas. It evolved from a gourdlike vegetable with bitter flesh but edible seeds. Remains of these seeds, dating as far back as 7000 to 5000 B.C., have been found in burial caves among Mexico's Tamaulipas Mountains. Pieces of stems, seeds, and shell have also been discovered in the ruins of ancient cliff dwellers of the southwestern United States.

The Native North Americans introduced early European settlers to the pumpkin. When half the Pilgrims died during their first arduous winter in the New World, the Patuxet Squanto showed the survivors how to reap an abundance of food by planting prolific pumpkin vines among corn, using herring as fertilizer.

In October 1621 the Pilgrims had cause for their first big celebration, and the pumpkin was featured as part of the feast. It was probably

3

boiled, although before long the settlers learned to make a simple pumpkin "pie" by removing the top, scooping out seeds and fibers, filling the cavity with milk, and roasting the pumpkin whole until the milk was absorbed.

The year 1622 offered no occasion for renewed celebration — the harvest was poor and the supply ships brought few provisions. To avert starvation, Governor William Bradford ordered the Pilgrims to grow more pumpkins.

Apparently, the plan worked: In 1623 the settlers held their second celebration. That off-again, on-again event eventually evolved into Thanksgiving Day, which today wouldn't be complete without pumpkin pie.

Pumpkins keep well in storage to provide sustenance throughout winter, adding to their importance as an early staple. They were such a common food during America's infancy that the Port of Boston was known as Pumpkinshire, and a Plymouth Colony poet wrote:

> *If fresh meat be wanting to fill up our dish*
> *We have carrots and pumpkins and turnips and fish;*
> *We have pumpkins at morning and pumpkins at noon;*
> *If it was not for pumpkins, we should be undone.*

Pioneers traveling westward carried along their pumpkin seeds, a practice attested to by the once common phrase, "As fat as a prairie pumpkin." Settlers became so fond of pumpkins that when they migrated to a place where their traditional pumpkins wouldn't grow, they adapted the nearest native squash and called it a pumpkin.

In tough times, pumpkin meat could be made into a substitute for such hard-to-get staples as flour, molasses, and sugar. The pumpkin was so ubiquitous at the family table that a circuit-riding preacher once prayed, "Dear Lord, give me just one good meal without pumpkin."

Englishman John Josselyn apparently didn't share this antipumpkin sentiment. In the late 1600s he visited New World farms and gardens, and in 1672 wrote in *New-England's Rarities Discovered* that pumpkins were a "pleasant food, boiled and buttered and seasoned with Spice."

Through selective breeding over the years, the stringy, watery, bland fruits of earlier times evolved into pumpkins with sweet, thick, smooth-textured meat. Pumpkins remained an important staple until after World War II, when refrigeration supplanted root cellars as a way to preserve out-of-season foods. Instead of a necessity of life, the pumpkin then became a symbol of bounty — something to be displayed on the front porch or carved for the amusement of children.

As families moved away from the country into suburban homes, many found their backyards too small to accommodate sprawling pumpkin vines. Those who continued enjoying pumpkins were less likely to grow their own than to buy them seasonally at grocery stores and roadside stands.

The pumpkins they bought, grown in fields measured by the acre, were not developed for their superior culinary properties, but instead for superior marketing qualities: hard shells and tough stems, flat roll-resistant bottoms, facelike symmetry, and a size that offered plenty of room for creative carving. As pumpkin carving has evolved into an art form, pumpkin growing has developed into an entertainment industry, complete with on-farm hayrides through the fields to seek out the season's perfect specimen.

Perfection, in this case, involves not only symmetry but also size. Intrigued by the possibilities, growers of giant pumpkins now engage in friendly but intense international competition. Rather than planting pumpkins by the field, competitive growers put in only one, or perhaps a few, pampered plants.

The flavor of pumpkins grown for size and/or for carving is secondary to their structural strength, and these "entertainment pumpkins" require a lot of space, so pumpkin growing hasn't been a top priority for gourmet cooks and kitchen gardeners. Indeed, many cooks and gardeners are totally unfamiliar with the sweet pumpkin, which is truly a connoisseur's delight.

But a combination of factors is changing all that: the evolution of gardening into a recreational pastime and the discovery that pumpkins can easily be grown, even by those who weren't born with a silver hoe in their hands; the development of compact varieties that take up less garden space; the desire to return to healthful home food production; and a burgeoning awareness of the importance of heirloom seeds, leading to a renewed appreciation of cultivars that are more suitable for culinary purposes than for carving. For all these reasons, pumpkins are more popular today than ever before, with new varieties introduced each year.

– 2 –
Fruit of Many Faces

Where the squash ends and the pumpkin begins is not only hard to determine, but a matter of fierce difference of opinion between squash/pumpkin fanciers. . . Even botanists have trouble identifying some specimens.

— Terry Pimsleur
The New Pumpkin Book, 1981

IT NEVER FAILS TO AMAZE ME that so many otherwise informed cooks or gardeners haven't a clue that a pumpkin suitable for carving doesn't necessarily make good eating, and vice versa. If I want to carve, I select a nicely shaped jack-o'-lantern pumpkin. If I want to cook, I select a sweet, meaty pie pumpkin. The two are worlds apart.

What Is a Pumpkin?

Life was simpler back when I was growing up. In those days we knew of only two kinds of pumpkin — the smallish kind with sweet, firm flesh that makes delicious pies, and the somewhat larger pumpkin, good only for carving into jack-o'-lanterns because of its hard shell and stringy,

7

watery meat. Today pumpkins come in a broader assortment, ranging from apple-sized miniatures, through globes of innumerable sizes, shapes, colors, and uses, and on up to gigantic record breakers that, to be moved, require a good half-dozen stout men. How can they *all* be pumpkins?

Determining what is, or is not, a pumpkin is a constant and hotly contested debate among pumpkin devotees. Some consider a pumpkin to be any fruit that's round and orange and a member of the squash family. Others insist that to qualify as a pumpkin, it must also have meaty flesh that's fine textured and flavorful enough to make outstanding pies.

Earlier in this century, a bunch of botanists thought they had settled the debate by defining a pumpkin as any fruit of the genus *Cucurbita* with a hard, ridged stem — in contrast to a squash, which (by their definition) has a soft, round stem. But that definition turned out to include several squash varieties that no one would consider calling pumpkins, so it was back to the drawing board.

Competitive vegetable growers stir the murky waters with their oversized, orange-shelled, meaty squashes, which they call giant pumpkins. To a competitive grower, if it's orange it's a pumpkin; if it's green it's a

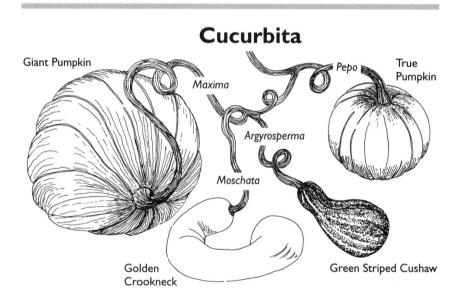

Cucurbita

Giant Pumpkin

Maxima

Pepo

True Pumpkin

Argyrosperma

Moschata

Golden Crookneck

Green Striped Cushaw

The pumpkin family tree.

squash. But that leaves out the 'White Jack-O-Lantern', the 'Green Striped Cushaw', the 'Queensland Blue', and the tan-shelled 'Cheese' pumpkin.

A Squash or a Berry?

So what *is* a pumpkin? No one disputes the fact that a pumpkin is not actually a vegetable but a fruit, and a berry at that. Like other berries, the pumpkin is a simple fruit that develops from a single pistil of the flower and has no stone (like a peach's) or papery core (like an apple's). Unlike other berries, however, the pumpkin has a hard outer shell.

Nor does anyone dispute the fact that pumpkins belong to the family Cucurbitaceae, consisting of 90 genera and 700 species of tender, heat-loving plants with tendril-bearing vines and alternate leaves. This family includes all cucumbers, melons, squash, and gourds. And everyone agrees that the pumpkin's genus is *Cucurbita,* which includes all varieties of pumpkin, gourd, and winter and summer squash. The controversy starts, however, when you get down to species. Of the six *Cucurbita* species, so-called pumpkins fall under four: *C. pepo, C. argyrosperma* (formerly *C. mixta), C. moschata,* and *C. maxima.*

In attempting to describe the relationships among these four species, Glenn Drowns of Calamus, Iowa, explains that "the big orange thing" everyone readily recognizes as a traditional pumpkin is a pepo. Pepos prefer northern climates that are frost-free from late April through early

October, but lack early-summer heat. A pumpkin of the pepo species has a hard, woody, ridged stem, and most have orange shells. Nonpumpkin pepos include acorn squash, spaghetti squash, summer squash, and hard-shelled gourds.

Glenn — who has been growing pumpkins since he was three years old and might well be the nation's leading authority on the subject — points out that as early settlers moved westward and brought along their pumpkin seeds, they sometimes found that C. pepo wouldn't grow well in the new area. They looked for something similar that *would* grow, and they called *that* a pumpkin.

In the South, the closest thing to a pepo that can withstand the insects running rampant in hot, humid weather is C. moschata, a species that includes one of the oldest cultivated pumpkins in the Americas, the 'Cheese' pumpkin. The 'Cheese' — so called because it's round and flat, like a wheel of cheese — is closely related to the butternut squash. The parent of the butternut is the 'Golden Cushaw' pumpkin, which, like the 'Cheese', has a tan shell and solid, sweet, orange meat.

In the hot, dry air of the Southwest, where nights stay warm, the 'Green Striped Cushaw' *(C. argyrosperma)* does well, so it's a "pumpkin" to southwesterners, even though it's by no means orange and its flesh tends to be thin and bland compared to that of other pumpkins.

The nearest thing to a pumpkin that tolerates the cool, wet weather of the North is C. maxima. The characteristics of this pumpkin — closely related to the banana and the hubbard squash — include a soft, spongy stem without ridges. All giant pumpkins are maximas, but not all maximas are huge. And not all maximas are orange. 'Lumina', the "painting pumpkin," is pearly white, and the drum-shaped 'Queensland' pumpkin is blue. It's called a pumpkin, however, because in Australia the word *pumpkin* means "squash." Some would insist that *all* maximas, regardless of their color, are squashes, simply because they aren't pepos.

Today's botanists argue that only a C. pepo is a "true" pumpkin and that all other species are technically varieties of winter squash. The rest of us have no trouble identifying members of all four *Cucurbita* species as pumpkins. As far as we're concerned, if it looks like a pumpkin or tastes like a pumpkin, it is a pumpkin.

The Four Types of Pumpkin

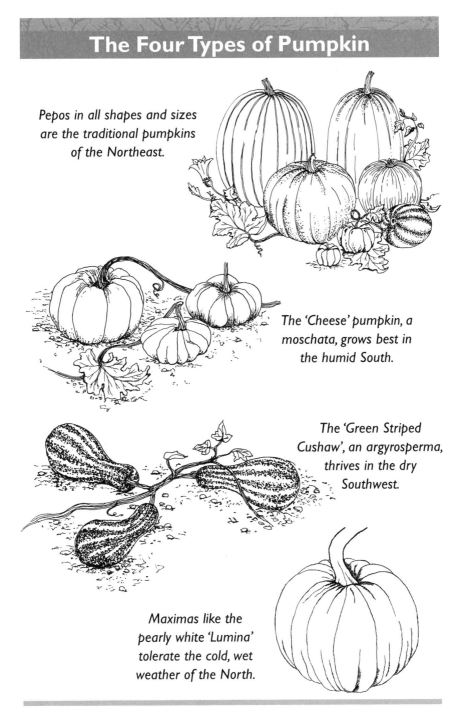

Pepos in all shapes and sizes are the traditional pumpkins of the Northeast.

The 'Cheese' pumpkin, a moschata, grows best in the humid South.

The 'Green Striped Cushaw', an argyrosperma, thrives in the dry Southwest.

Maximas like the pearly white 'Lumina' tolerate the cold, wet weather of the North.

Ornamental Miniatures

The miniature pumpkin was developed by Colorado's Hollar Seeds, but very nearly never saw the light of day, because neighbors kept sneaking over to "liberate" the cute little pumpkins from their vines in the growing fields. In desperation, the grower moved his test site to a location he kept secret from everyone, including Hollar executives.

Miniature pumpkins are popular with children because the small fruits are easy for little hands to handle.

Introduced as the 'Sweetie Pie' by Stokes Seeds, the mini is now sold under other names, including 'Munchkin' and its most common and graphic designation, 'Jack-Be-Little'. Measuring 3 inches (7 cm) across and weighing only a few ounces, this mini is a sellout success at farmstands and florist's shops because it's just the right size for holiday centerpieces. Some people believe minis are too small to be worth eating, but I find them tasty and attractive when baked and served, one per person, in their own jackets.

Despite the fruit's small size, the vines range widely, even stretching up into low-growing trees. One year I planted some in my orchard and ended up with little orange pumpkins hanging from the lower limbs of a dwarf apple tree. As you might guess, these vines are ideal for growing on trellises.

Since the original miniature came out, a spate of others has followed, including the ghost white 'Baby Boo'; the compact, vining 'Jack-B-Quick' (suitable for growing in confined spaces); and the larger, rounder 'Little Lantern', sometimes called 'Baby Pam'. All miniatures are pepos.

Culinary Pumpkins

A good cooking pumpkin is not only sweet and firm fleshed, but also a good keeper. If you're looking for a pumpkin to grow strictly for culinary purposes, consider one of the heirloom varieties. You won't go far wrong with a 'Small Sugar' or 'Winter Luxury' (both pepos), a 'Cheese' pumpkin or 'Golden Cushaw' (both moschata), or a 'Rouge Vif d'Etampes' (a maxima). Most newer varieties fall short of these in both flavor and texture.

Pumpkin Characteristics

	Maxima	Argyrosperma	Moschata	Pepo
VINES	very long	spreading	spreading	spreading (some compact)
LEAVES	huge, hairy rounded jagged edges barely lobed slightly blotchy	large, hairy triangular rounded tips barely lobed blotchy (greener than mosch.)	large, hairy triangular pointed tips barely lobed blotchy (darker than argyros.)	prickly triangular jagged edges very lobed blotchy
STEM	spongy/corky hairy circular retracts at fruit attachment	hard hairy slightly angular flares slightly before retracting at fruit attachment	hard hairy slightly angular flares before retracting at fruit attachment	hard prickly angular (5 sides) angles continue into fruit
BLOSSOMS	narrow petals	leaflike petals	large, leafy green sepals at base	narrow petals
SHELL	shiny	matte (bloom)	matte (bloom)	shiny
SEEDS	thick white, tan, or brown light margin paper-thin coat	cracked white or tan pale margin paper-thin coat	small beige dark, ragged margin	smooth ivory pale margin

maxima — 'Dill's Atlantic Giant'

argyrosperma — 'Cushaw'

moschata — 'Cheese'

pepo — 'Baby Pam' / 'Small Sugar'

For northerners, *the* pie pumpkin is the 'Small Sugar', a variety that goes by many names, including 'New England Pie', 'Northern Pie', and 'Sugar Pie'. Sugar pumpkins weigh in the 5- to 8-pound (2.3–3.6 kg) range and are famous for their sweet, solid, fine-grained flesh.

In my southern garden the small 'Sugar' pumpkin ripens too early for winter storage, but I grow it anyway because the vines are prolific and I like the flavor of the flesh, which also remains firm in pickles and preserves. Glenn Drowns, on the other hand, swears by the 'Winter Luxury'.

The 'Cheese' pumpkin and the 'Golden Cushaw' (sometimes called the Neck pumpkin after its long, curved, flesh-filled neck) are both good choices for growing in hot, humid climates. Moschatas, in general, have the sweetest meat of all the pumpkins. Commercially, more pies are made from moschatas than from pepos.

The 'Rouge Vif d'Étampes' was popular in French markets in the 1800s and has since come back home to North America. Its shape is somewhat similar to that of the 'Cheese' pumpkin, but its shell is ruddier in color. It, too, goes by several different names, including the 'Cinderella' (because it was the original model for Cinderella's coach) and the 'Deep Red' (after the color of its shell).

This is by no means an exhaustive list of culinary pumpkins. Others are available regionally, developed to grow well under local conditions. Still others are generated by seed companies as "improved" varieties. Do your homework when selecting a variety for your kitchen garden. Some great-sounding pumpkins (the 'Spookie', for example) are actually intermediate between culinary types and carving types, and are truly outstanding for neither.

Many cooks consider the heirloom Sugar pumpkin to be the only variety suitable for pies and other culinary dishes.

Jack-o'-Lanterns

Carving-type pumpkins are grown less for their flavor than for their attractive appearance and the sturdiness of their stems. As a result, their flesh tends to be bland and watery. Their culinary properties don't matter much, though, since once a pumpkin has been carved, its meat is ruined for eating.

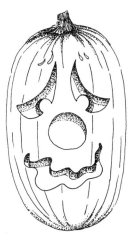

Any pumpkin can be carved, provided it has enough structural strength to withstand holes cut into its shell. A flat bottom is also an asset, so your displayed creation won't roll. Although you should never carry a pumpkin by its stem (lest the stem break off and the fruit subsequently rot), a good jack-o'-lantern has a strong stem that makes a sturdy lid handle.

A traditional carving variety is symmetrical and has a flat bottom.

Carving pumpkins are generally large, to allow plenty of space for design development, and are roundish rather than flattened — although some carvers prefer elongated pumpkins taller than they are wide. A symmetrical shape is preferred by some, while others enjoy the challenge offered by irregular proportions.

Since 1871 the standard carving pumpkin has been the heirloom pepo 'Connecticut Field', a variety that ranges in size from 15 to 30 pounds (6.8–13.6 kg) and is not always uniform in shape. The 'Howden Field', developed by Jack A. Howden as an improvement upon the 'Connecticut Field', is more uniform in size and shape, and is more symmetrical. It also has thicker flesh and is therefore less likely to grow lopsided.

A number of other variations on the 'Connecticut Field' and 'Howden' have been developed, many of them bearing Halloweenish names such as the 'Ghost Rider' and 'Jack-O-Lantern'. Some varieties, developed to be planted in backyard gardens, grow on compact vines that take up less space than the widely spreading vines of commercial field pumpkins.

Some carving pumpkins, notably the 'Autumn Gold' and its cousin the 'Big Autumn', carry a precocious yellow B gene that turns the shell from green to golden before the pumpkin is fully ripe. This characteristic is appreciated by commercial-scale growers, who harvest and market early, and by those whose growing season is short.

In warm, humid climates, the moschata 'Southern Field' is best suited to the Halloween pumpkin patch. Crafters who prefer longer-lasting painted artwork to a short-lived carving, however, may opt for a white-shelled maxima such as the 'White Jack-O-Lantern' or Burpee's 'Lumina'.

Giant pumpkins present giant carving challenges. Their shells are tough (especially toward the stem end) and their flesh thick, sometimes as thick as 8 inches (20 cm). Still, while a maxima like 'Dill's Atlantic Giant', 'Big Max', or 'Prizewinner' takes longer to carve than a pepo, the result can be truly magnificent.

Giant Pumpkins

Giant pumpkins are grown primarily for displays and contests. All giant pumpkins are maximas, the largest fruits in the plant kingdom. The biggest of the lot is 'Dill's Atlantic Giant', developed by Howard Dill of Nova Scotia. During the last quarter of the 20th century, the world-record weight for a pumpkin has more than doubled — from 451 pounds (203 kg) in 1976 to 1,061 pounds (478 kg) in 1996. In comparison, baby giants such as the 'Big Max' and 'Big Moon' weigh a mere 200 pounds (90 kg) or less.

Due to their great weight, giant pumpkins tend to get flat on the side that rests against the soil, giving them a not-very-pumpkinlike appearance. To make matters worse, the shell has a bleached-out yellowish or pinkish color, rather than the bright orange you would expect of a proper pumpkin. Still, giant pumpkins are spectacular for their size alone.

Like any pumpkins, giants may be eaten. Like carving varieties, however, they tend to be watery and bland, although some are finer fleshed than others.

Like 'Prizewinner', all giant pumpkins are maximas.

Naked Seed Pumpkins

Naked seed pumpkins produce seeds without hulls, a handy trait if you like snacking on fresh-roasted pumpkin seeds but don't enjoy cracking shells between your teeth. Until recent years, commercially grown pumpkin seeds sold as snack foods were hulled by hand in Mexico or China. Thanks to dedicated pumpkin propagators, though, seeds now come right out of the pumpkin practically ready to eat. Instead of a tough hull, they're covered with only thin film. Some pumpkin varieties, called semi-hull-less, have seeds with thin, rudimentary hulls.

As handy as naked seeds are for eating, at planting time they germinate less well than hulled seeds, and they rot more readily in cool soil. Since hull-less pumpkins are grown primarily for their seeds, they tend to have only a thin layer of flesh.

The varieties 'Lady Godiva' and 'Naked Seed' have been around a long time. Newer varieties are bred to have larger seed cavities (hence less meat and more seeds) and to grow on compact vines. University of New Hampshire horticulturist Brent Loy is responsible for developing the 1- to 2-pound (0.45–0.9 kg) 'Snackjack', a compact-vining plant with fruits yielding 300 to 400 seeds each, or about 1,500 pounds (681 kg) of seeds per acre. He then genetically enlarged the seeds to about the size of Spanish peanuts. The 'Snackjack', like all naked seed pumpkins, is a pepo.

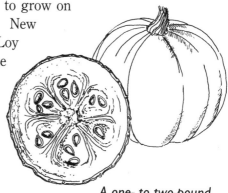

A one- to two-pound 'Snackjack' has a large cavity with 300 to 400 hull-less seeds.

Stock Feed

Surplus pumpkins make great feed for cattle, sheep, goats, pigs, or poultry. The raw pumpkin is cut or chopped into pieces of appropriate size for the animal being fed. Animals that are unfamiliar with pumpkins, though, need time to get used to them. Although no one has done a study on the matter, anecdotal evidence indicates that pumpkins may be more readily relished by minor breeds (which have retained an instinct to forage) than by modern hybrids (bred to thrive on formulated rations).

Some livestock owners grow pumpkins expressly for feed. The larger carving varieties (the 'Connecticut Field' and 'Kentucky Field') and the smaller of the giants (the 'King Mammoth Gold') are the ones most often grown for this purpose. In warm climates Cushaws are more suitable for feed — the 'Green Striped' where the air is dry, and the 'Golden' where conditions are humid.

Heirlooms and Hybrids

Unless you're lucky enough to live near a farmstand that offers lots of variety by way of pumpkins, you'll likely have little choice in what you buy. Grocery stores generally carry only two kinds of pumpkin: miniatures for fall decorating and jack-o'-lanterns for Halloween carving. If you grow your own, however, your choice is unlimited.

In selecting seed, you'll naturally base your choice first on the characteristics of the fruit. Other things to consider are the growth habits of the vine, the average number of days from sowing the seed to fruit maturity, and whether or not the variety is open-pollinated.

Open-pollinated (OP) seeds are produced by flowers that are pollinated by natural means — bees, insects, and sometimes wind. The seed from an open-pollinated variety may be saved and planted from year to year. All heirloom varieties, many of them dating back a century or more, are open-pollinated. *Heirlooms* often accumulate several names over time, perhaps given to them by local growers who forgot or never knew the original name, or perhaps applied to a strain selectively bred to perform well under local conditions. Different strains behave in different ways, depending on both the selective process under which they are propagated and the conditions under which they are grown.

As a general rule, heirlooms are hardier than newer varieties, more resistant to insects, and more flavorful. Growing them ensures their continuing availability to gardeners, which in turn helps ensure genetic diversity.

OP Hybrids

Not all OP varieties are heirlooms. Some have been propagated more recently, developed by crossing two different varieties or species through hand pollination (as described beginning on page 61). The resulting hybrid offspring are selected for their desirable characteristics, such as compactness of the vine, short maturation time, or resistance to disease. Through repeated reproduction, these characteristics become fixed, resulting in a new OP variety that represents some improvement upon (or novel change from) either original parent.

If you grow an OP hybrid, you can save its seed from year to year for replanting; these hybrids, like heirlooms, therefore contribute to bio-diversity. Some have the initials PVP attached to them, meaning their propagators have been granted a U.S. certificate of Plant Variety Protection. Seed from certified plants cannot legally be propagated for sale by anyone other than the PVP holder or an entity (business or per-son) designated by the PVP holder. OP varieties that are not PVP certi-fied may be propagated and sold by anyone, and often appear in different seed catalogs under different names.

First-Generation Hybrids

Varieties designated F_1 are also hybrids, developed by crossing two different varieties or species. In this case, though, they are first-genera-tion hybrids; F_1 stands for first filial, filial meaning "offspring." First-generation plants are genetically uniform and exhibit hybrid vigor, but they are not stable — their seeds will not produce uniform plants or fruit. Second-generation plants may vary widely or revert back to one of the parent types. Saving seed from an F_1 hybrid is therefore a waste of time. If you want to grow pumpkins just like the original F_1 hybrids, you must recross plants like the parents.

The genetically different parent plants of an F_1 hybrid are them-selves highly inbred and thus closely guarded by their propagators. Their seed production may be PVP certified. Ostensible reasons for propagating F_1 hybrids include development of vines that are compact, prolific, and disease resistant and produce uniform fruits that transport easily.

But the genetic uniformity of F_1 plants makes them vulnerable to crop failure, an important consideration for commercial growers. Furthermore, by concentrating genetic resources, hybridization both contributes to genetic erosion and ensures our dependence on seed com-panies, rather than on our own resources. For these reasons, many seed sellers carry only OP varieties, some specializing solely in heirlooms.

Variety	OP/F$_1$/PVP*	Species	Growth Habit
MINI			
'Baby Boo' (Stokes)	OP/PVP	*C. pepo*	vining
'Jack-B-Quick'	OP	*C. pepo*	semicompact 10–12'
'Little Gem' (Africa) 'African Gem'; 'Gem'	OP	*C. pepo*	vining
'Sweetie Pie' (heirloom) 'Halloween'; 'Jack-Be-Little'; 'Munchkin'	OP	*C. pepo*	semicompact 10–12'
CULINARY			
'Acoma' (heirloom)	OP	*C. pepo*	vining 8'
'Ancestors' (heirloom)	OP	*C. pepo*	vining
'Baby Bear' (Johnny's Selected Seeds)	OP/PVP	*C. pepo*	semicompact 10–15'
'Big Cheese' (heirloom) 'Magdalena Big Cheese'	OP	*C. moschata*	vining
'Big Red California' (heirloom)	OP	*C. pepo*	vining
'Buckskin'	F$_1$	*C. moschata*	vining

*OP = Open-pollinated; F$_1$ = F$_1$ hybrid; PVP = Plant Variety Protection
**Varies with local growing conditions

Days to Maturity**	Size	Other Characteristics
95–100	4–6 oz. 3"D 2"H	White-shelled version of Sweetie Pie; 10 fruits per vine; shapes vary; crosses readily with gourds; sweet white flesh.
95	4 oz. 3"D 2"H	Similar to 'Jack-Be-Little' but smaller, taller, deeper orange shell, and more ribbed, more uniform fruits.
90–100	4 oz. 3"D 2"H	Round; early yellow; bright orange shell; keeps well.
90–100	3–4 oz. 3"D 2"H	8–10 fruits per vine; resists powdery mildew; flattened, deeply grooved, deep orange shell; strong stem; small seed cavity; sweet flesh; keeps well.
90–95	10–15 lbs.	1,000-year-old variety from Sky City pueblo, bluish shell; thick, fine-textured flesh; keeps well.
100	10–12 lbs.	Ribbed, warty shell.
120	1.5–2.5 lbs. 6"D 4"H	6–8 fruits per vine; resists fusarium and gummy stem blight; tolerates fall frost; round, somewhat flattened, smooth, deep orange shell; long twisted stem; seminaked seeds; fine-grained flesh; stores 12–16 weeks.
125	50 lbs.	Grows well in hot climates; ribbed, flattened, light orange to tan shell; sweet, bright orange, nonstringy flesh; keeps well.
80–90	3–4 lbs.	Deep orange shell; 1"-thick yellow flesh.
115	12 lbs. 7"D 10"H	Acorn-shaped, buff-colored shell.

Variety	OP/F$_1$/PVP*	Species	Growth Habit
CULINARY cont'd.			
'Bushkin' (Burpee)	OP/PVP	*C. pepo*	compact 5–6'
'Cheese'	OP	*C. moschata*	vining
'Cinderella'	OP	*C. pepo*	compact 5'
'Connecticut Sweet Pie' (heirloom)	OP	*C. pepo*	vining
'Cushaw, Golden' (heirloom) 'Golden Crookneck'; 'Golden Cushaw Pumpkin'; 'Mammoth Golden Cushaw'	OP	*C. moschata*	vining
'Cushaw, Green Striped' 'Striped Crookneck'; 'Striped Cushaw' (Caribbean heirloom)	OP	*C. argyrosperma*	vining
'Cushaw, White'	OP	*C. argyrosperma*	vining
'Flat White' 'Flat White Boer'	OP	*C. maxima*	vining
'Idaho Gem' (Drowns)	OP	*C. pepo*	semicompact
'Japanese Pie'	OP	*C. argyrosperma*	semicompact
'Kentucky Field Long'	OP	*C. moschata*	vining
'Little Lantern' (Stokes)	OP	*C. pepo*	vining

Days to Maturity**	Size	Other Characteristics
95	8–10 lbs.	1–3 fruits per vine; bright orange shell; thick, light yellow flesh.
120-125	10 lbs.	Tan shell, tall cheese-box shape; orange flesh; keeps well.
95	7–15 lbs. 10"D	2–3 fruits per vine.
95	6–8 lbs.	Taller than wide.
90–120	6–12 lbs. 9"D 18–20"L 4–5"neck	Parent of 'Butternut' squash; smooth, hard, tan to yellow-orange shell with curved neck; solid, sweet, dry flesh; keeps well.
75–115	12–16 lbs. 8–10"D 16–20"L	Prolific; drought and heat tolerant; resists vine borer and cucumber beetle; pear-shaped with long, curved neck; mottled green-striped hard, thin, smooth, creamy white shell; thick, fine-grained, pale yellow, moist, sweet flesh, mostly in neck.
90–100	10–20 lbs.	Crookneck type; pale creamy flesh.
110	5–10 lbs.	Flattened white shell; thick, sweet, dry, yellow flesh; keeps well.
80	4–6 lbs.	Similar to 'Sugar Pie' but earlier maturing; softer flesh does not keep well.
110	10–15 lbs.	Hard, dark green shell, thick stem, pale orange-yellow, sweet, nutty flesh; stores well for up to 6 months.
125	35–40+ lbs.	Oblong, blocky, smooth, tan shell; deep orange flesh.
100	5"D 5½"H	Prolific; uniform, smooth, scarcely ribbed shell; tightly secured 5" stem; deep orange-yellow flesh.

Variety	OP/F$_1$/PVP*	Species	Growth Habit
CULINARY cont'd.			
'Long Cheese'	OP	*C. moschata*	vining
'Long Pie' (heirloom)	OP	*C. pepo*	vining
'Minnesota Sweet' (heirloom)	OP	*C. pepo*	vining
'My Best Pie' (heirloom)	OP	*C. maxima*	vining
'Neck Pumpkin' (heirloom)	OP	*C. moschata*	vining
'Northern Bush' (Fisher's)	OP	*C. pepo*	compact
'Papaya Pumpkin' (Asia)	OP	*C. moschata*	vining
'Rouge Vif d'Étampes' 'Cinderella' (French heirloom); 'Deep Red d'Étampes'; 'Étampes'; 'French Heirloom'; 'Red Étampes'; 'Rouge d'Étampes'	OP	*C. maxima*	vining 15'
'Seminole' (Everglades heirloom)	OP	*O. moschata*	spreading vine
'Small Sugar' (heirloom) 'Boston Pie'; 'Classic Pie'; 'Early Northern Pie'; 'Early Sugar Pie'; 'Early Sweet'; 'Early Sweet Pie'; 'New England Pie'; 'Northeast Pie'; 'Northern Pie'; 'Small Sweet'; 'Sugar'; 'Sugar Pie'; 'Sweet'	OP	*C. pepo*	semicompact

Days to Maturity**	Size	Other Characteristics
125	20-30 lbs.	Flattened, tan shell; dark orange flesh; keeps well.
110–120	12"L	Zucchini-shaped deep orange shell; 1"-thick orange flesh.
100–110	2-4 lbs.	Dark orange, thick shell; 1"-thick, pale orange flesh.
105	10-20 lbs.	Blocky, deep pink, lightly ribbed shell; 3"-thick, pale orange flesh.
120	18–24"	Forerunner of 'Butternut' squash; long crookneck; thick, solid, dry, sweet flesh.
90	5–8 lbs.	Cross between Cheyenne Bush and Orange Winter Luxury; deep orange shell; thick, fine-grained, golden-yellow flesh.
90	2 lbs.	Looks like a papaya; sweet, thick flesh with nutlike flavor.
95–110	25–30 lbs. 15"D 6–8"H	Flattened, deeply grooved, shiny, rough, red-orange shell; thick, red, sweet, moist rich-tasting flesh; keeps well.
130	8–10 lbs. 6–8"D	Prolific, insect resistant; grows well in wet or dry climates; hard, buff-colored shell; sweet flesh.
90–115	6–8 lbs. 7–8"D	Prolific; resists black rot; slightly flat, round, thick, hard, orange shell; thick, sweet, bright orange, smooth-textured, dry, nearly stringless flesh; good keeper.

Variety	OP/F₁/PVP*	Species	Growth Habit

CULINARY cont'd.

Variety	OP/F$_1$/PVP*	Species	Growth Habit
'Spookie' 'Deep Sugar Pie'; 'Improved Sugar Pie'; 'Spookie Pie'	OP	*C. pepo*	vining
'Spooktacular' (Petoseed)	F$_1$	*C. pepo*	vining
'Storage' (heirloom)	OP	*C. pepo*	vining
'Sugar Baby' (heirloom)	OP	*C. pepo*	spreading vine
'Sugar Treat' (Rupp)	F$_1$	*C. pepo*	compact
'Whangaparoa Crown'	OP	*C. maxima*	vining
'White Rind Sugar' (heirloom)	OP	*C. moschata*	vining
'Winter Luxury' (heirloom) 'Luxury Pie'; 'Queen'	OP	*C. pepo*	vining
'Yellow Large Paris' (France) 'Jaune Gros de Paris'	OP	*C. maxima*	vining
'Young's Beauty'	OP	*C. pepo*	spreading vine

NAKED SEED

Variety	OP/F$_1$/PVP*	Species	Growth Habit
'Lady Godiva' (heirloom) 'Hulless'	OP	*C. pepo*	vining 8–10'

Days to Maturity**	Size	Other Characteristics
90–110	6–10 lbs. 6–7"D	'Sugar Pie' crossed with 'Jack-O-Lantern'; prolific; resists black rot; sizes vary; bright orange, lightly ribbed, semismooth, hard, red-orange shell; strong stem; thick, smooth-textured, firm, sweet, yellow-orange flesh.
85	3–5 lbs. 6"D 5"H	Early yellow 'Baby Pam' hybrid; prolific; deep orange shell; uniform size and shape; strong stem; fine-textured flesh.
90	5–7 lbs.	Similar to 'Small Sugar' but taller and with thicker skin; good keeper.
95	4–6 lbs. 3"H 8"D	Prolific; disease resistant; distinct ribbing; sweet, orange flesh.
90	4–5 lbs. 5"D	'Baby Pam' hybrid; strong stem; slightly ribbed, deep orange shell.
120	6–8 lbs.	Hard grey shell with crown top; small seed cavity; deep orange, dry, sweet flesh; keeps well.
130	5–8 lbs.	White shell; solid flesh.
100	8 lbs. 10"D	Prolific; nearly round, golden-russet shell, finely netted when ripe; yellow flesh; good keeper.
105	40–60 lbs.	Large, pinkish-yellow shell; sometimes flattened in shape.
120	8–12 lbs. 8"D	Large 'Sugar Pie' type; prolific; resists black rot; hard, medium-ribbed, uniform, dark orange shell; thick stem; thick, sweet, yellow-orange flesh.
100–105	8–12 lbs.	12–15 fruits per vine; green shell; greenish seeds; harvest when cracks appear in stem.

Variety	OP/F$_1$/PVP*	Species	Growth Habit
NAKED SEED cont'd.			
'Godiva Hulless Bush'	OP	*C. pepo*	semicompact
'Naked Seed' (heirloom)	OP	*C. pepo*	vining
'Mini-Jack' (Stokes)	OP	*C. pepo*	vining
'Snackjack' (Loy, U.N.H.)	F$_1$	*C. pepo*	compact 4–5'
'Styrian Hulless' (Austria)	OP	*C. pepo*	spreading vine
'Triple Treat' (Burpee)	OP/PVP	*C. pepo*	spreading vine
'Trick or Treat' (Petoseed)	F$_1$	*C. pepo*	semicompact 12–15'
CARVING & ORNAMENTAL			
'Appalachian' (Petoseed)	F$_1$	*C. pepo*	compact
'Aspen' (Hollar)	F$_1$	*C. pepo*	compact
'Autumn Gold'	F$_1$	*C. pepo*	semicompact 12–20'
'Big Autumn'	F$_1$	*C. pepo*	semicompact
'Bloomfield' (heirloom)	OP	*C. pepo*	vining

Days to Maturity**	Size	Other Characteristics
100	8–12 lbs.	Compact-vine version of 'Lady Godiva'.
80–85	1–3 lbs.	Bright orange, thinly ribbed shell; 1"-yellow flesh; grown commercially to be pressed for salad oil.
115	1–1½ lbs. 4–6"D	Prolific; hard, round, orange shell; greenish seeds; thin flesh.
90–100	1–2 lbs.	Large seed cavity, numerous seeds; thin flesh.
100–120	20 lbs.	Green shell; high-quality seeds.
110	6–8 lbs. 7–9"D	Round, deep orange shell; medium-textured, thick, deep orange flesh; keeps well.
105–110	10–15 lbs. 11"D 14"H	Similar to 'Cheyenne' but larger; taller than wide; non-uniform size; strong stem; lightly ribbed, dark orange shell; thick flesh.
90–100	25 lbs.	Similar to 'Happy Jack'; high yields; uniform fruit; strong stem; dark orange shell.
90–100	15–20 lbs. 9–12"D	Similar to 'Howden' but smaller; strong stem; rich orange shell with medium ribs.
90–100	10–15 lbs. 10–12"D	3–5 fruits per vine; uniform size and shape; round; early yellow; smooth, glossy, bright golden-orange, lightly ribbed shell; strong stems; thick flesh.
90–100	15–20 lbs. 12–15"D	30% bigger than 'Autumn Gold'; early, strong stem; uniform round to oblong symmetrical shape; smooth, ribbed, light-colored shell; deep orange flesh.
100–110	15–30 lbs.	Strong stem; thick, deep orange flesh.

Variety	OP/F$_1$/PVP*	Species	Growth Habit
CARVING & ORNAMENTAL cont'd.			
'Casper'	OP	*C. pepo*	vining
'Cinderella'	OP	*C. pepo*	compact 6'
'Connecticut Field' (heirloom) 'Big Tom'; 'Jaune de Champs'; 'Southern Field'; 'Yankee Cow'	OP	*C. pepo*	spreading vine
'Frosty'	F$_1$	*C. pepo*	compact
'Funny Face'	F$_1$	*C. pepo*	compact 5'
'Ghost Rider' (Burpee)	OP	*C. pepo*	spreading vine
'Golden Oval' (heirloom)	OP	*C. pepo*	vining
'Gold Rush' (Rupp)	OP/PVP	*C. pepo*	vining
'Half Moon' (Petoseed) 'Half Moon Long Yellow'	OP	*C. pepo*	spreading vine
'Happy Jack'	OP	*C. pepo*	spreading vine
'Harvest Moon' 'Seneca Harvest Moon'	F$_1$	*C. pepo*	compact

Days to Maturity**	Size	Other Characteristics
90	10–20 lbs. 8"D 10"H	Smooth, white shell.
84–95	7 lbs. 10–12"	Round, uniform, bright orange shell; needs especially well-drained soil; does not keep well.
100–120	15–30 lbs. 10–14"H 12–15+"D	Not uniform in size and shape; hard, thin, smooth, slightly ridged, deep gold-orange shell; round with flattened ends; thick, sturdy stem; thick, sweet, coarse, dry, orange-yellow flesh.
90–95	10–15 lbs. 10"D	Prolific; small-stemmed; ribbed but smooth, bright orange shell of uniform color.
100	10–15 lbs. 11"D 14"H	Prolific; uniform size, shape, and color; light orange, rough, lightly ribbed shell; thick flesh; moderate keeper.
110–115	15–30 lbs.	Similar to 'Howden' but smaller; uniform, dark orange, smooth, lightly ribbed, hard, round shell with dark, tough stem; yellow-orange flesh.
90–95	6–10 lbs.	Flattened shape; unusual color—sometimes orange-and-yellow striped.
120	30–40 lbs.	Round, deep orange shell; thick, strong stem; thick, dark-orange flesh.
105–115	12–15 lbs. 14"D	Tall 'Connecticut Field' type; not easy to grow; readily sunburns; dark orange shell; strong stem; thick, dark yellow, coarse flesh; named after Half Moon Bay, California's pumpkin capital.
105–110	10–20 lbs. 12"H	'Howden' type; uniform size; strong stem; smooth, lightly ribbed, dark orange shell.
90–100	10–20 lbs. 12–15"D	Roundish, deep orange shell; strong stem.

Variety	OP/F$_1$/PVP*	Species	Growth Habit
CARVING & ORNAMENTAL cont'd.			
'Howden' (Howden) 'Howden Field'	OP/PVP	*C. pepo*	spreading vine
'Jack-O-Lantern' 'Halloween'	OP	*C. pepo*	spreading vine
'Jack of All Trades' (Hollar)	F$_1$	*C. pepo*	compact
'Jackpot' (Harris)	F$_1$	*C. pepo*	semicompact
'Jumpin Jack' (Rupp)	OP/PVP	*C. pepo*	spreading vine
'Kumi Kumi' (New Zealand heirloom)	OP	*C. pepo*	vining
'Little Boo' (Agway) 'Painting'	OP/PVP	*C. pepo*	vining
'Lumina' (Burpee)	F$_1$/PVP	*C. maxima*	vining 20'
'Mother Lode' (Rupp)	F$_1$	*C. pepo*	semicompact
'Northern Gold' (Fisher's)	OP	*C. pepo*	semicompact

Days to Maturity**	Size	Other Characteristics
110–115	15–20 lbs.	Improved 'Connecticut Field'—larger, more uniform in size and shape; prolific; resists black rot; round, symmetrical, hard, deep orange shell with flat face; thick but poor-quality flesh; keeps well; popular commercial carving pumpkin.
100–115	10–18 lbs. 7–10"H 7–10"D	'Connecticut Field' crossed with 'Golden Oblong', originated in Minnesota, designed to be "the size of a man's head"; poor stem; shape varies; round, smooth, barely grooved, bright-orange, firm shell with flattened ends; thick, fine-grained, pale yellow flesh; keeps well.
88–90	9–10 lbs. 8–9"D	Vigorous vines; strong stem; uniform fruit; smooth, slightly ribbed, dark orange shell.
100	10+"D	Prolific; uniform size; round, yellow-orange, smooth shell; strong stem.
110–120	40–50 lbs.	Similar to 'Howden' but larger; taller than wide, dark orange, smooth, slightly ribbed shell; dark, solid stem; thick, dense, deep orange flesh.
120–125	4–6 lbs.	Ribbed, tough shell, great for decorating; 1"-thick yellow flesh is sweet, but stringy and difficult to extract.
105	6–8 lbs.	Gourdlike pumpkin with smooth, hard, white shell, good for painting and decorating.
80–90	10–20 lbs. 8–10"D	Creamy white, glossy, nearly round shell retains color if harvested while immature; bright orange, tasty flesh; good keeper.
90–100	20–30 lbs.	Similar to 'Jumpin Jack' but more prolific, more uniform, and earlier; strong stem.
90	7–10 lbs.	Early yellow; sweet, deep orange flesh.

Variety	OP/F$_1$/PVP*	Species	Growth Habit
CARVING & ORNAMENTAL cont'd.			
'Pankow's Field'	OP	*C. pepo*	vining
'Peek a Boo'	F$_1$	*C. pepo*	vining
'Southern Field' 'Dickinson'; 'Kentucky Field'	OP	*C. moschata*	spreading vine
'Southern Miner' (heirloom)	OP	*C. pepo*	vining
'Spirit'	F$_1$	*C. pepo*	compact 4–5'
'Tallman' (Stokes)	OP	*C. pepo*	vining
'Thomas Halloween'	OP	*C. pepo*	spreading vine
'Trickster'	F$_1$	*C. pepo*	compact
'Turner' (heirloom)	OP	*C. pepo*	vining
'Wizard'	F$_1$	*C. pepo*	semi compact
'Xochitlan Pueblo' (Mexican heirloom)	OP	*C. pepo*	vining

Days to Maturity**	Size	Other Characteristics
100–115	18–22 lbs.	'Howden' type but smoother, more variable in shape and color; round to tall, symmetrical shell; supersturdy stem; extra thick flesh.
90–100	4 lbs. 6"D 5"H	Uniform size and shape; long, dark green stem; deep orange shell.
120–130	25 lbs.	Flattened, globe-shaped, slightly ribbed, bright yellow-orange shell; sweet, deep-yellow flesh.
120–125	4–6 lbs.	Similar to 'Kumi Kumi'; mottled green to yellow, wide-ridged, tough shell great for decorating; 1"-thick yellow flesh is difficult to extract.
90–110	10–15 lbs. 12"D 14"H	Similar to 'Jackpot'; prolific; uniform size; symmetrical, oblong, smooth, bright orange shell; strong stem; thick, yellow flesh; moderate keeper.
110	15–30 lbs. 16"H	Resists powdery mildew; upright shape; hard, slightly ribbed, deep orange shell.
110	15–30 lbs.	Resists black rot; sturdy stem; hard, slightly ribbed, deep orange shell; thick flesh.
90–100	3 lbs. 9"D	High yielding; strong stem; deep orange shell.
100–110	10–15 lbs.	Strong stem; hard, ribbed, deep orange shell.
110–120	10–15 lbs.	Prolific; strong stem; darkest orange, smooth-ribbed shell.
80–85	2–4 lbs.	Prolific; smooth, hard shell that tends to split in rain when fruit is ripe; 1"-thick yellow flesh.

Variety	OP/F₁/PVP*	Species	Growth Habit

GIANT

Variety	OP/F₁/PVP*	Species	Growth Habit
'Dill's Atlantic Giant' (Dill) 'Giant Pumpkin'	OP/PVP	*C. maxima*	spreading vine 50'
'Big Max' 'Big Mac'; 'Big Mack'; 'Great pumpkin'; 'Jumbo'; 'Pink Giant'	OP	*C. maxima*	spreading vine
'Big Moon' (Petoseed)	OP/PVP	*C. maxima*	spreading vine
'Boston Marrow' (heirloom)	OP	*C. maxima*	spreading vine
'King Mammoth Gold' 'Kentucky Large Field'; 'King of Mammoths'	OP	*C. maxima*	spreading vine
'Mammoth Gold' (heirloom) 'Mammoth'; 'Mammoth Orange Gold'; 'Pot Iron'	OP	*C. pepo*	spreading vine
'Prizewinner' (Burpee)	F₁	*C. maxima*	spreading vine
'Queensland Blue' **(Australian heirloom)**	OP	*C. maxima*	spreading vine

Days to Maturity**	Size	Other Characteristics
120–130	500+ lbs. 10' circ.	World record holder; yellow to orange shell; tends to flatten on ground side; thick, meaty, orange flesh.
110–120	100+ lbs. 17–18"D	Round to flattened, rough, pinkish shell; uniform shape, strong for carving; 3–4"-thick, fine-grained, yellow-orange flesh.
110–120	40–200+lbs. 40"D	Similar to 'Mammoth Gold'; 1–2 fruits per vine; resists powdery mildew; slightly rough-textured, evenly ribbed, golden-orange shell; large, brown seeds; thick, fine-textured, light orange flesh; named after Half Moon Bay, California's pumpkin capital.
95–100	10–12 lbs.	Dark orange-red shell; teardrop shape; moist orange flesh.
105–130	50–75 lbs.	Large version of 'Mammoth Gold'.
105–110	20–25 lbs.	Prolific; irregular globe, flattened on bottom; slightly ribbed, smooth, deep yellow shell, mottled with orange, sometimes netted; solid, coarse flesh.
120	50–200 lbs.	Nice round shape despite its size; smooth, shiny, dark reddish orange, shallow-ribbed shell; small stem; good for carving.
110–120	80 lbs.	Drum-shaped, ribbed, slate blue shell; keeps well.

– 3 –
The Pumpkin Patch

*P*umpkins are the most nearly animal of the garden vegetables; watching over their progress through a season is like watching a calf come along.

— Castle W. Freeman Jr.
Country Journal, 1980

PUMPKINS GROW IN ALL AREAS of North America and are among the easiest vegetables to start from seed. And while they offer easy rewards for the novice, they can also offer challenging demands for the expert.

When to Plant

Pumpkins are a long-season crop, usually requiring 90 to 120 growing days, depending on the variety you plant and the summer's temperature. If your growing season is short, plant one of the early-maturing varieties, or plant seeds indoors (as described beginning on page 45) and transplant the seedlings after the danger of frost has past. If your growing season is long, you may plant a rapidly maturing variety later in the season, but the vines won't produce as much fruit and will be more susceptible to disease and drought stress than early-grown vines.

Pumpkins are also a warm-season crop. To sprout, the seeds require a soil temperature of no less than 60°F (16°C). The warmer the soil, the faster the seedlings will burst into life. Once sprouted, the tender young seedlings are easily damaged by frost.

The ideal daytime temperature for growing vines is 80 to 85°F (27–29°C); the ideal nighttime temperature is 60 to 65°F (16–18°C). Vines can tolerate cooler nights, provided the temperature remains above freezing — pumpkin vines are extremely frost-tender.

Pumpkins should be planted as soon as the danger of frost is past and the soil is suitably warm. Depending on the part of the country you live in, ideal pumpkin-planting time can range from the beginning of March to the beginning of June. Two rules of thumb:

- Plant pumpkin seeds when blackberries start to bloom.
- Soil that's warm enough to sprout corn is warm enough to sprout pumpkin seeds.

Where to Plant

Just how much sun your pumpkins need depends on the species you grow and your location. All pumpkin species like full sun in their native climates — pepos and maximas in Temperate Zones, argyrospermas and moschatas in hot climates. If you grow pepos or maximas in the South or Southwest, plant them in semishade to protect their leaves from drying out or scorching. Even so, hot weather causes pepos to mature early, can ruin their flavor, and in the extreme will kill the vines.

Soil Temperature and Germination

Minimum	60°F	16°C
Optimum range	70–95°F	21–35°C
Optimum	90°F	32°C
Maximum	100°F	38°C

Unfavorable conditions for all species include extreme temperature fluctuations during the season (which can ruin flavor and texture), less than half a day of full sun throughout the season, and fog or wind during the better part of the summer. Pumpkin vines have big leaves that easily dry out in wind. Protect your vines from occasional winds by planting them near taller plants or along a fencerow, or by erecting a windbreak.

PUMPKINS LIKE:
- Sun
- Protection from wind
- Plenty of space
- Rich, well-drained soil
- Neutral or acid pH

Saving Space

The only complaint I've ever heard about pumpkins is that they take up too much garden space. The runners of a ranging variety may spread 15 feet (4.5 m) or more in all directions. Crowding plants together isn't the answer; the result will be fewer and smaller fruits.

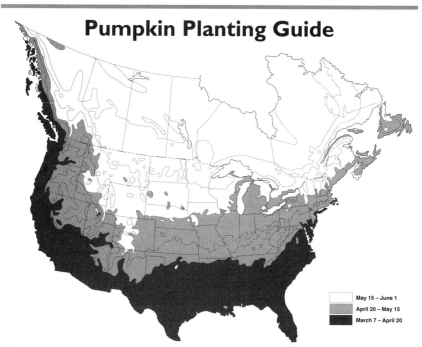

Pumpkin Planting Guide

☐ May 15 – June 1
▨ April 20 – May 15
■ March 7 – April 20

Ideal pumpkin-planting time can range from the beginning of March to the beginning of June, depending on where you live.

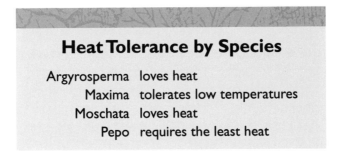

Heat Tolerance by Species

Argyrosperma	loves heat
Maxima	tolerates low temperatures
Moschata	loves heat
Pepo	requires the least heat

You can control the spreading growth habits of pumpkin vines in six ways:

1. Use the space-saving trick Pilgrims learned from the Native Americans — grow pumpkins among rows of corn. This option is described more fully beginning on page 55.

2. Plant vines at the edge or the uphill end of your garden, to give runners more room to roam.

3. Trellis varieties with small- to midsized fruit. Miniature pumpkins take well to trellising. Larger fruits must be hung in slings fashioned from stretchy hosiery, so they won't break off the vine. Large jack-o'-lantern pumpkins and giant pumpkins, of course, are too heavy for trellising.

Trellising has several advantages besides saving space. Fruits grown off the ground have a more uniform color, are less likely to be blemished by insects, and are less likely to rot due to contact with damp ground. Vines have less exposure to soilborne diseases and are less likely to get stepped on. (However, since a trellised vine has less contact with soil, it can't put down the extra roots that would help it resist vine borer.)

4. Plant a compact variety; these require as little as one-third the space of a vining type. Compact varieties are often called bush or semi-bush, even though they don't really bush in the same way that a zucchini plant does. You'll get fewer pumpkins from a compact vine, but they will be the same size as the fruits of similar varieties with spreading growth habits. Compact vines have shorter runners and smaller leaves than standard varieties. They also have fewer leaves to photosynthesize food, so they require especially fertile soil.

5. When vines begin to sprawl, you can control their spread by *gently* turning back the tips. But take care — the hollow vines kink easily, and when that happens the stem stops transporting moisture and nutrients from the roots to the leaves and fruits. Runners are easiest to move without damage after they have been warmed several hours by the sun.

6. Pinch back longer (6–8 foot, or 180–240 cm) runners after fruits begin to grow. One year our vigorous Winter Luxury vine stretched its runners toward our electric fence. To keep the fence from shorting out (thus delighting rabbits, deer, and groundhogs), we frequently mowed the fence line clear. Our efforts seemed not to adversely affect the harvest, for that year we had more pumpkins than ever.

How to Plant

When I lived in northern California, I planted pumpkin seeds in staggered wells spaced close enough together that the vines rapidly grew into a dense thicket of leaves to shade the soil, keeping moisture in and weeds out. All I did was plant, mulch, and wait until autumn to harvest my crop.

Here in Tennessee my pumpkins require much more care, partly because summers tend to be droughty and partly because we have more insects and plant diseases to contend with. I now grow pumpkins in one long row of wells, giving me easy access to the vines from both sides.

Pumpkins may be planted in four ways: hills, wells, rows, and intensive beds.

Hills

Hills are favored by organic growers because compost and rotted manure need to be worked only into each hill, not into the surrounding soil. Hills improve drainage and help the soil warm more rapidly in spring. A hill is a flat mound of soil, 2 to 3 feet (60–90 cm) in diameter, raised a few inches (cm) above the surrounding soil.

Space hills 8 to 10 feet (2.4–3 m) apart, depending on the vining habits of the variety you plan to grow. For compact varieties, space hills 4 to 6 feet (1.2–2 m) apart. Each standard vine will spread to a diameter of 25 feet (750 cm); compact vines can grow to 12 feet (360 cm). Plants should eventually overlap to shade out weeds. Until they do, minimize weed growth and dry soil by spreading a generous layer of clean straw or other mulch.

At the center of each hill form a shallow depression. Space three or four seeds around the depression, 1 inch (2.5 cm) deep, and cover with fine soil. Don't *pack* soil over the seeds, though, or you'll deprive them of the oxygen they need to grow.

When seedlings reach about 2 inches (5 cm) in height, pull or pinch all but the strongest one in each hill. Some growers leave two or three seedlings per hill, but since pumpkins are heavy feeders they will compete against each other and none will do really well. You may, if you wish, hedge your bets and initially leave an extra plant or two growing in each hill, *pinching* out the extras when one clearly emerges as the strongest. Do not, at that point, *pull* out the extras, or you'll run the risk of disturbing the roots of the plant you leave behind.

To plant seeds, form separate soil hills with a shallow depression in the center of each. Place 3–4 seeds about 1" deep into each depression.

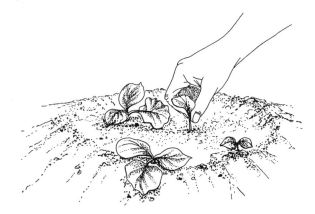

After seedlings get their first true leaves, remove all but the strongest in each hill.

Wells

Wells, or inverted hills, are depressions made at soil level, created by removing soil from the center of a circle and heaping it around the rim. Since our Tennessee soil tends to dry out rapidly, we find that wells collect and retain moisture better than hills.

Rows

Rows are generally favored by market growers, because they're more conducive to mechanical cultivation. One way to create rows is to mound loose soil into raised beds (think of each as a long, continuous hill), planting seeds in a series of wells along the center. Space rows 8 feet (2.4 m) apart for vigorous vines, 6 feet (1.8 m) for a less rangy variety, and 5 feet (1.5 m) for compact vines. Plant seeds 12 inches (30 cm) apart in each row. When the seedlings develop true leaves — plants will be 4 to 6 inches (10–15 cm) tall — thin to one plant every 5 feet (1.5 m) for a variety with vigorously spreading vines, 3 feet (90 cm) for semicompact vines, and 2 feet (60 cm) for compact vines. Thin gradually, in case you lose some plants.

Intensive Beds

Intensive beds are not often planted to pumpkins, due to the vines' wide-ranging habits. But if you prefer to grow intensively, compact or bush vines are best suited. You'll get fewer fruits per plant, but more from the total plot than you would get with conventional spacing. By spacing seeds 30 inches (75 cm) apart in a zigzag pattern, you can grow up to a dozen vines in a standard 4-foot by 20-foot (1.2 by 6 m) bed, from which you can expect about 60 pounds (27 kg) of pumpkin. You may turn back wandering vines as they grow, trim off tips that stray out, or train some of the runners to grow on trellises.

Tip for Rapid Growth

To provide steady moisture and stimulate rapid growth of seedlings, poke a series of small holes in the bottom of a gallon jug, partially bury the jug in the center of a hill or well, and plant seeds around the jug. Fill the jug daily with water.

Starting Seeds Indoors

To get a jump start on the growing season, sow your pumpkin seeds indoors. Starting seeds indoors is an especially good idea if:

- Your growing season is short
- Your spring weather rapidly turns hot and dry (as ours does here in Tennessee)
- You want mature pumpkins in time to enter fairs and festivals occurring in early fall

Compared to seeds planted outdoors, those started indoors have a better germination rate, because they're sprouted under controlled conditions. To start your own indoor nursery, you'll need:

Seeds. Decide what kind of pumpkins you want to grow and purchase the seeds in plenty of time. (A list of mail-order sources appears at the back of this book.)

Containers. Those of us who enjoy indoor planting invariably set up in-house recycling centers filled with containers suitable for starting seeds. To avoid disturbing roots at transplant time, the best containers for pumpkins are either tapered (like yogurt cartons) so plants can be easily slipped out, or made of paper (like milk cartons) that can readily be torn open for plant removal. Although flats (shallow trays) offer more planting space than individual pots, removing seedlings from them is difficult without disturbing roots.

Since pumpkin seedlings grow more rapidly than many other garden vegetables, and their roots get thick and long, they should be started in quart-size or gallon-size containers. To prepare the containers for planting, wash them well, rinse them in warm water laced with a little chlorine bleach, and dry them in the sun. With a nail, poke one or more small drainage holes in the bottom of each container so you won't drown your seedlings.

If money is no object, avoid the bother of saving and cleaning containers by buying pots designed for sprouting seeds. Seedlings started in pots of pressed fiber or peat can be planted in the garden, pot and all, without disturbing fussy little roots.

Planting mix. Seeds sprout best in soil that drains well, doesn't easily compact, and is free of competing weed seeds, fungi, and other organisms that can sicken young plants. Sterile planting mixes, available at any garden center, are relatively inexpensive. If you buy a mix containing soil, be sure the label says it's been sterilized.

Most mixes blended especially for germinating seeds contain no soil at all, but are a combination of sphagnum moss (decomposed moss mined from swamps), perlite (a form of volcanic ash), and vermiculite (mica expanded with heat, like popcorn). This blend holds water well but is difficult initially to moisten. To dampen it sufficiently for planting, put some into a plastic bag, add water, and knead. Because such a mix is low in nutrients, you'll have to fertilize seedlings from the time they achieve three weeks' growth, using half the strength of whatever solution you'd use for mature plants.

Homemade Planting Mix

Make your own planting mix by combining equal parts sphagnum moss, sifted compost, and sifted garden soil. The sphagnum moss holds moisture, the compost contributes nutrients, and the soil binds them together. To eliminate soilborne bacteria and fungi that can cause plant problems, mix the soil and compost and pasteurize them in one of three ways:

1. Spread the mix thinly in a clean flat and liberally pour boiling water over it.
2. Moisten the mix, put it in a large plastic pot, put the pot inside a clear plastic bag, seal the bag tightly, and set it in the sun for two weeks.
3. Lightly moisten the mix (steam does the sterilizing) and heat it in a 180°F (82°C) oven for 45 minutes. Since roasting soil doesn't exactly smell like fresh-baked bread, place the mix in a broiler bag (of the sort you'd use to cook a turkey) and spread it on a shallow pan.

Cool the sterilized mix, rub it through a screen to loosen lumps, and stir in the sphagnum moss.

Labels. If you start more than one variety of pumpkin, labels will help you keep track of what's what. They'll also tell you which variety to replant if some pots don't sprout. You can buy bona fide nursery labels, save up Popsicle sticks, or make labels by cutting a liquid bleach container into ½-inch (1 cm) vertical strips and trimming one end into a point. Some planting containers (such as cartons from yogurt, cottage cheese, and sour cream) are easy to write on with an indelible marker, eliminating the need for separate labels.

Warmth. Pumpkin seeds sprout best in a warm, draft-free place. If the temperature is too low — below 60°F (16°C) — the seeds will rot. A suitably warm place might be the top of the water heater or refrigerator, or near a radiator or furnace vent. After the seeds germinate, move the pots under a light.

Light. Seedlings grown on a windowsill soon get leggy and topple over. A light fixture for your seedlings therefore makes a good investment and can be used year after year. You might enjoy the prestige (and expense) of a grow-light, but you'll get the same good results with inexpensive fluorescent tubes and a fixture from the local discount store.

Cool white ("daylight") 40-watt tubes throw even light of the sort plants thrive on, and they don't get hot enough to burn tender leaves. Select a fixture (or fixtures in combination) the right size to cover all the pots directly beneath it. Hang the fixture from chains so you can raise it as plants grow, keeping it just above the leaftops without touching them. Some growers run their light 12 to 18 hours per day and turn it off at night, on the theory that plants need a rest; we leave ours on all the time and always get top-quality transplants.

Procedure

Start pumpkin seeds no more than two weeks before the last expected frost date in your area, when you can safely transplant them to the garden. To ensure that your garden soil will be warm enough for the transplants, cover your pumpkin plot with black plastic about the same time you start your seeds indoors. If you aren't sure of your area's last frost date, call your county's Cooperative Extension Service office. Timing is important since pumpkins grow fast, and if plants become spindly or rootbound in their pots, they won't do well when transplanted.

Fill each container with planting mix to within 1 inch (2.5 cm) of the top. Press the mix gently, to firm it up without packing it solid. In each container, arrange two seeds, pointed end down. Cover with 1 inch (2.5 cm) of soil. Water well and keep the mix evenly moist. To avoid washing planting mix away from the seeds, water the pots with a spray bottle filled with warm water. Keep the soil from drying out by laying a piece of newspaper, plastic wrap, or waxed paper across the tops of the containers. Water the pots daily, taking care to let the soil get neither soggy nor dry.

The seeds should germinate in about 5 days in soil at 75 to 85°F (24–29°C); or 7 to 10 days if your soil is cooler. As soon as the first thick, flat "seed" leaves appear, remove the paper cover and turn on the grow-light. Keep the plants well lighted and at a daytime temperature of 75°F (24°C); the nighttime temperature should be no less than 60°F (16°C). Continue watering daily to keep the soil evenly moist.

About two weeks after a seed sprouts, you should see the vine's first true leaves — vaguely heart shaped with jagged edges. When plants have four true leaves (not counting those first nondescript seed leaves), thin the seedlings to one per pot. Don't pull out the weak plants or you'll disturb the roots of the remaining plant. Instead, use scissors to snip off the weaker seedling at soil level. Water a little less often from now on, allowing the soil's surface to dry out between waterings. Your seedlings are ready to be transplanted anytime now.

Sprouting Problems

Legginess is a common problem in seedlings started indoors. Long, weak stems may be caused by excessive temperature, too little light, or overcrowding so that seedlings have to compete for light. I've never had much luck overcoming legginess once it occurs. The trick is to prevent it in the first place by growing seedlings where the temperature is no higher than 85°F (29°C), keeping them under a fluorescent light (not on a windowsill), planting them in individual pots, and pinching or cutting out all but one plant per pot.

Damping off is another common problem of seedlings started indoors. You know you have a damping-off problem when stems shrivel up at soil level, and seedlings flop over and die. Damping off may also kill newly sprouted seedlings that haven't yet broken through the soil's surface. For more on damping off, see page 115.

Failure to sprout may occur not only due to damping off, but also if the soil is too cold, too hot, or too dry; if the seeds were planted more than 1 inch (2.5 cm) deep; or if the seeds were old or improperly stored (see "Saving Seeds," on page 66). Giant and naked seed varieties have an inherent tendency to germinate poorly — giant seeds because of their tough hulls, naked seeds because without protective hulls, they're more susceptible to rotting.

To improve the germination rate of giant seeds, you can soften the hulls by soaking the seeds for 24 hours in warm water; or, try weakening the hulls by lightly filing or sandpapering both ends. Presprouting will improve the germination rate of both giant-pumpkin and hull-less varieties.

Presprouting

Sprouting pumpkin seeds before you plant them improves their germination rate and helps them germinate more quickly. Layer together two or three moistened paper towels or napkins, space seeds on the towels so they don't touch, then carefully roll up the towels and place them in a plastic bag. Put the plastic bag in a warm place, such as on top of the water heater or refrigerator, where the temperature is close to 75°F (24°C). Check the seeds daily. In four or five days, each will sprout a "tail" — the new plant's root. As soon as the root appears, place the seed in a pot or plant it outdoors, root end downward. Be careful, the new root is brittle and breaks off easily.

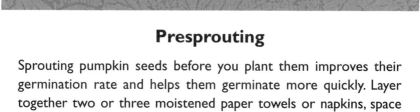

Transplanting

Pumpkin seedlings grow amazingly fast, and can quickly outgrow their pots while you're waiting for conditions outside to be just right for the big move. If that happens, transplant them into larger pots. The move will stimulate root growth, thanks to new soil with fresh nutrients and greater room for roots to spread. Work gently, since pumpkin seedlings don't like to have their roots disturbed.

Whenever you transplant a seedling, here's the procedure: First, thoroughly water it. Then run a butter knife around the edge of the pot to loosen the rootball. Hold the pot in one hand and tip it upside down onto your other hand, so the rootball lands on your fingers with the plant stem between them. (If you started the seeds in fiber or peat pots, simply break away the bottom so the roots can get through, then plant, pot and all.) In the new location, add enough planting mix to bury the stem up to the first true leaves. Press the mix firmly around the roots and water the plant once more. Transplants may droop at first, but should return to upright within a day.

When the time comes to move your plants outdoors, avoid an abrupt move that will shock them and retard their growth. Instead, let the vines gradually adjust to being outside through a process called *hardening off.* One week before transplant time, place the pots outdoors in a shady spot that's protected from wind (potted seedlings are highly vulnerable to drying out). Bring the pots inside before the sun goes down.

After a couple of days you can leave them out overnight if nighttime temperatures don't drop below 40°F (4°C). Gradually move the pots each day until the plants get full sun throughout the day. Watch that your seedlings don't get dried out from the sun or wind; you may have to water them more often than you have been.

Transplant the seedlings into the garden only after all danger of frost has past. Plant them at least as deep as they were in the pots. If more than 1 inch (2.5 cm) of stem shows below the first leaves, heap soil around it to encourage new root growth. If the seedlings are in peat pots, don't forget to tear off the bottoms or poke holes in each pot so the roots have no trouble expanding. Make sure peat pots are entirely covered with soil, too, or else the portion above ground will act as a wick, evaporating moisture from the pot to create an impenetrable wall roots can't break through.

To transplant, tip the pot, gently holding the plant stem between your fingers, until the rootball slides out, landing against the palm of your hand.

For peat pots to work most effectively, the bottoms have to be removed and the top edges completely covered by soil.

Protecting Seedlings

The best time to move seedlings to the garden is on a warm, windless, cloudy day when light showers are predicted. Unfortunately, the weather doesn't always cooperate. Chilly nights, not to mention the drying effects of wind and sun or the damaging effects of a late frost, can wipe out all those little vines you tended so carefully.

Garden centers carry protective devices of every shape, size, and — especially — price. Hot caps hold in heat during the night but must be removed on sunny days so they won't collect the sun's heat and cook your new transplants. An option is Wall-o-Water protectors, which absorb heat

In this homemade wall of water, 2-liter soda bottles have been laced together, encircling the vine.

during the daytime and slowly release it at night. For a homemade substitute, fill 2-liter soda bottles with water, place them in a circle around each vine, and lace them together with twine. Another low-cost option is to make a miniature cold frame by cutting the bottoms from gallon-sized plastic milk jugs; to release the heat generated by the sun, remove the caps from the jugs during the day.

If you have tomato cages, cover them with clear plastic and use them as hot caps. By the time you need the cages for tomatoes, they'll no longer be needed by the pumpkin vines.

Floating row covers — light sheets of polypropylene — are another option. They can be removed when summer temperatures heat up or, in a year-round cool climate, they can be supported — creating a tunnel — and left on all summer. When the flowers bloom, lift the covers to allow pollination. The ends of the tunnel must also be opened up for ventilation during summer's hottest days; letting plants overheat, or letting evaporation gather beneath covers, encourages disease.

Hay bales or trellising, placed around vines and draped with burlap, will hold in warmth at night. If you have nothing else at hand when frost threatens, place a couple of stakes on either side of each seedling and slip an inverted paper bag over them in late afternoon, before the sun goes down. If wind threatens to blow, put a small stone or dirt clot on top of each bag to keep it from blowing away. Be sure to remove the bags in the morning, soon after the sun comes up, to avoid trapping excess heat.

No matter what type of protective device you use, arrange it so it doesn't touch the tender leaves.

Pumpkin Cultivation

Unless you're trying to beat the world record for growing the biggest pumpkin (the subject of chapter 4), your vines need little pampering. As members of the same family as cucumbers, melons, squash, and gourds, they require similar growing conditions. Alas, they are also attacked by many of the same insects and diseases (the subject of chapter 5).

Since pumpkins are heavy feeders, and since weeds compete with them for soil nutrients, cultivate as often as necessary to keep down weeds. But remember that along each runner pumpkins put down an extensive system of feeder roots — roots that remain close to the soil's surface. Weed only by hand to avoid damaging them.

Mulching

Those of us who don't have much time for weeding prefer to discourage weeds by mulching. A layer of shavings or clean straw 3 to 4 inches (7.5–10 cm) deep deters weed growth, helps retain soil moisture, and protects fruits from soil-borne diseases that cause rot. If you garden in a warm climate, spread mulch early in the season, before vines start to run.

In cool climates, a mulch of shavings or straw applied too early in the season keeps the ground from heating up, and applied late in the season may prevent the soil's residual heat from warming the plants at night. To

A good layer of mulch deters weeds and helps the soil retain moisture.

overcome these problems, use plastic sheet mulch, which serves the same purposes as natural mulch but in addition draws heat from the sun to warm the underlying soil. Its chief disadvantage is that it doesn't let runners put down roots unless you poke a hole through the sheet under each leaf stem. Alternatively, use dark-colored mulch like peat or cocoa bean hulls to absorb the sun's heat.

Fertilizer

For good root development, vines require well-drained, well-aerated soil, preferably sandy or loamy. As garden vegetables go, pumpkins are heavy feeders, meaning they consume a lot of nutrients during the season. They grow best in humus-rich soil with balanced fertility. Good soil fertility is especially important for compact vines, which have fewer leaves for photosynthesis. All pumpkin vines like soil that's acidic (pH 6.0) to nearly neutral (pH 7.0). If your soil is too high in acid (below pH 6.0), sweeten your pumpkin patch with crushed eggshells or dolomitic limestone.

As the season progresses, the vine's nutrient needs change. Early on, vines need nitrogen for good leaf growth, but excessive nitrogen at this age will give you a big plant with nice dark leaves and no fruit set. A vine's nitrogen needs go up later in the season, after fruit has set, because cucurbits photosynthesize more rapidly while bearing fruit.

For nice plants with large fruit, apply at least 2 inches (5 cm) of well-rotted manure or compost in the fall, working it into the upper 6 to 8 inches (15–20 cm) of soil. You may instead apply manure in early spring, several weeks before planting time, but use only well-rotted manure to avoid burning plants; if it smells, it's too hot. If you prefer using chemical fertilizer, apply 2 to 4 pounds of 10–10–10 or 15–15–15 per 100 square feet (1–2 kg/10 sq. m). Every three weeks during the growing season, sidedress with compost, rotted manure, or 5–10–5 fertilizer, or water with fish emulsion.

Tip for Symmetrical Growth

If you want your maturing pumpkins to have a nice symmetrical shape, rotate them occasionally so the side against the ground won't get flat. Turn each pumpkin only a little at a time, though, taking care not to bend or break the brittle vine.

An easy way to ensure that your vine gets enough nutrients is to plant seeds on top of an old compost heap. If you don't happen to have an old compost heap, pile up manure at the edge of your garden in the fall and plant seeds on top in spring. As the vines spread and put down more roots into the heap, they will obtain increasingly more nutrients as the season progresses. After the harvest, spread the manure over your whole garden and start a new pile for next year.

FERTILIZER/WATER

Pumpkins are heavy feeders. During the growing season, sidedress your vines every three weeks with compost, rotted manure, 5-10-5, or fish emulsion and keep the soil evenly moist.

Water

Because pumpkin vines have hollow stems and large leaves, they're sensitive to drying out, especially while they're flowering and fruiting. Don't ever let the soil get completely dry. Initially, apply water all around each vine, extending well beyond the main root. After the vines become established, avoid root rot by applying water all around *but not on or near* the main root. Unless rainfall is at least 1 inch (2.5 cm) a week, thoroughly water the soil once a week to a depth of no less than 4 inches (10 cm).

Water early in the day to minimize the spread of bacteria and fungi. Apply water only to the soil, never to the leaves or vines. If you must use overhead sprinklers, early-morning watering is especially important, to give leaves time to dry out before evening.

If vines are allowed to wilt due to lack of water, they'll produce smaller fruits. Too little, or too much, water can also cause fruits to turn soft and fall off the vine. If your problem is excessively moist soil, keep your growing pumpkins from rotting by placing them on boards.

The Three Sisters

An Iroquois legend tells how, when the Great Spirit walked across the earth, corn sprouted from her footsteps, beans appeared by her left hand, and pumpkins grew by her right hand. The Pilgrims learned from the Native Americans to grow together what the Natives came to call the three sisters: corn, beans, and squash.

Today the practice is called multicropping or polyculture. Interestingly, the sisters not only cooperate with one another to provide a more favorable growing environment for all three, but eaten in combination they provide a balanced diet for humans.

If you sow seeds of all three crops in the same hole together, the faster-growing beans and pumpkins will choke out the slower-growing corn. So give the corn a head start by planting it first; when stalks are about 18 inches (45 cm) high, plant pole beans and pumpkins. Sow the beans at the base of the corn to give them a place to climb, but space the pumpkins as you normally would, to keep them from overrunning the corn and beans. (*Warning:* Do not plant pumpkins with corn where southern corn rootworm is a problem; the adult version is a cucumber beetle that blemishes pumpkin shells and spreads disease.)

The three sisters work together as companion plants in many ways. Growing wide-spreading pumpkin vines among vertically oriented corn and beans saves space. Cornstalks give beans a place to grow, and shade pumpkins during hot summer days (but die back in time to let in sunlight for the fruits to mature). Pumpkin vines shade the soil to deter weeds, minimize soil erosion, and reduce evaporation of moisture from the earth. Although corn and pumpkins are both heavy feeders, corn feeds near the surface while pumpkins glean nutrients from deeper down in the soil; beans, meanwhile, enrich the soil for future crops. And the three sisters together create an environment that discourages pests: Pumpkin vines repel corn ear borer, and the prickly leaves discourage raccoons from getting into the corn.

As companion plants pumpkins, beans, and corn work together in many ways.

Pumpkin Companions

Good	Reason
Borage, lemon balm	Attract bees for good pollination
Clover	Keeps down weeds and enriches the soil when strip-cropped between pumpkin rows
Corn, sunflowers	Tall plants provide vines with natural wind-break; sprawly vines among tall crops save space and act as a living mulch (but do not plant pumpkins with corn where southern corn rootworms thrive)
Petunias, nasturtiums	Repel squash bugs
Radishes	Deter cucumber beetles when planted in a circle around each hill, one week before pumpkin seeds or at the same time as pre-sprouted seed
Zucchini	Lure squash bugs away from pumpkins

Poor	Reason
Cucumbers	Attract cucumber beetles, which spread diseases from vine to vine
Potatoes	Inhibit vine and fruit growth; potatoes become more susceptible to blight
Raspberries	Increase pumpkins' susceptibility to blight

Moon Phases

My father used to laugh at my grandmother for planting by the moon, but modern research is proving what gardeners have known from time immemorial — that the moon's phases affect the success of various gardening activities. Planting according to moon phases may very well maximize the productivity of your pumpkin patch, if for no other reason than that it increases your awareness of the forces of nature.

If you aren't acquainted with the phases of the moon, here's a run-down: The first two phases, or quarters, occur during times of increasing light, or when the moon is waxing; the first quarter runs from the new moon to the half-full moon, the second quarter runs from the half-full moon to the full moon. The last two phases occur during times of decreasing light, or when the moon is waning; the third quarter runs from the full moon to the half-full moon, the fourth quarter runs from the half-full moon to the new moon.

Pumpkins and the Moon

Garden Activity	Moon Phase
Plant (for fruit)	first quarter
Plant (for seeds)	second quarter
Pollinate	second quarter
Fertilize	third or fourth quarter
Prune vines	third quarter
Cultivate, weed, control pests	fourth quarter
Harvest	third or fourth quarter

Zodiac Signs

As the moon circles the earth, the 12 signs of the zodiac occur in sequence. Each remains in effect for two or three days and each purportedly affects plant growth. To maximize your efforts, plan pumpkin activities for those times when the appropriate zodiac sign coincides with the appropriate moon phase. To determine a day's sign, consult an *astrological* calendar, which may differ from an *astronomical* calendar.

Each of the signs governs some aspect of fertility. Cancer, for example, is a fertile sign, while Leo is barren. The best signs under which to conduct nearly all pumpkin-growing activities are the water signs: Cancer, Scorpio, and Pisces. Of these, Scorpio offers the best time to prune vines for improved fruit production. Two exceptions to the water-sign rule are: Weed and cultivate under Aries, Gemini, Virgo, or Aquarius; harvest under any sign *but* Cancer, Scorpio, and Pisces.

Regardless of the moon phase or zodiac sign, always use common sense. It won't do to plant pumpkins in frozen soil or postpone the harvest until after a heavy frost just to follow the moon and signs.

Sex and the Single Pumpkin

One of the intriguing things about pumpkins (and other members of the squash family) is that they are *monoecious,* meaning each plant has both male and female blossoms. The first blossoms appear in early July. Don't be alarmed when they wither and drop off without setting fruit. These first flowers are all males.

Enticing Bees

Bees must visit each pumpkin blossom several times for good fruit set. Highly pollinated blossoms will give you an abundant harvest of nicely shaped fruits. Entice bees to visit your vines by planting borage, lemon balm, or other herbs bees love among or near your vines.

If too few bees visit your pumpkin patch, move hives closer. One or two colonies per acre is sufficient. If you use toxic sprays to ward off insects, avoid poisoning the bees by applying insecticides late in the afternoon after blossoms have closed.

Soon female blossoms will appear. Only the female bears fruit. You can readily identify a female blossom as having what looks like a bulging baby pumpkin — the ovary — at its base. A male blossom sits on a straight, thin stem with no round bulge at the base.

A new male blossom appears almost daily. A new female opens only about every 7 to 10 days. Overall, a vine produces fewer female flowers than males — the ratio is about 1 female for every 15 to 20 males.

A female blossom that is not pollinated won't bear fruit. If you have plenty of bees around, they'll visit both male and female flowers and do the pollinating for you. But bees may also carry pollen from squash or other pumpkin varieties growing nearby. While this cross-pollination won't affect your fruit the first year, seeds saved from the cross and sown the second year may not bear the type of fruit you expect. If you plan to save seeds, you'll need to hand-pollinate to guarantee their genetic purity.

Other reasons to hand-pollinate:

- To ensure pollination if weather is too unfavorable for bees to leave their hives (rainy or too cool)
- To ensure complete pollination, for well-shaped fruit
- For maximum harvest
- To make sure a male blossom opens at the same time as a female blossom — a consideration if you grow only one vine
- To get bigger pumpkins — the more pollen is transferred, the bigger the fruit (and the more seeds it contains)
- To place fruits in favorable locations on the vine — a consideration when you grow giant pumpkins

A male pumpkin blossom (left) has a straight stem. A female pumpkin blossom (right) has a bulb-shaped ovary at its base.

Hand Pollination

Hand pollination is most successful in the cool of the morning, but preparations must be made the evening before. If you want to make sure bees don't beat you to the punch the next morning, go out in the evening and locate blossoms that are about to open. A developing blossom has a little color along its seams, and its tip is just beginning to come apart. Flowers that have already opened are no longer of any use for selective pollination.

1. As you select the male and female blossoms you intend to use, cover them with cheesecloth or seal their tips with yarn or masking tape that's sticky enough not to come loose in the morning dew. Clearly mark female blossoms with stakes so you can readily spot them.

   The males may be from the same vine as the female, or from a different vine. Pollination with males from the same vine is called selfing, and is desirable when you want to fix specific plant characteristics or if you question the genetic purity of other plants. Pollination with males from a different plant of the same variety is called sibbing, and results in a greater degree of genetic diversity.

2. In the morning pick a male flower, along with several inches (cm) of stem. Remove the tape or yarn and carefully strip off all the petals.

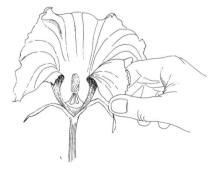

3. Unseal a female; the blossom will slowly open. Pollinate it by holding the stem of the male, as you would hold a brush, and gently rubbing the pollen-laden, rodlike male stamen against each section of the sticky stigma in the middle of the female flower. Pollination is more successful if you use more than one male for each female. Prepare five males before you open a female, so insects won't have time to sneak in while you go for another male.

4. If your goal is to prevent cross-pollination, when you're done reseal the female with yarn, tape, or cheese-cloth to exclude bees and other insects. If your goal is solely to ensure complete pollination, though, leave the female flower open to further pollination by bees.

Mark the stem of each blossom you pollinate, to help you readily identify it in case naturally pollinated fruits appear. If you grow more than one variety of pumpkin, tag each blossom and use an indelible marker to note the variety and the date. Otherwise, an easy-to-see colored tag is sufficient. Surveyor's ribbon is easy to see, but is often carried off by wildlife. Spiral bandettes, designed for identifying chickens, make ideal markers because they're colorful enough to see and they expand as stems grow.

Pollen travels down through the female flower into the bulbing ovary, where it joins an ovule to become a developing pumpkin seed. After the female has been pollinated — its ovaries fertilized — the blossom petals (designed solely to attract insects) dry up and fall off.

Potential Pollination Problems

Problem	Solution
A brittle blossom splits along its seams, leaving an opening where insects may enter.	Wrap masking tape down the blossom to cover the split, or cover the whole blossom in cheesecloth loosely tied at the bottom.
Bumblebees chew through the blossom to get the pollinate.	In the future wrap blossoms in masking tape or cover them loosely with cheesecloth.
The neck between the base of the flower and the fruit becomes damaged.	None — this fruit will abort.
Fruits abort (a particular problem for maxima growers).	Keep trying.
Poor pollination causes the blossom end of the pumpkin to shrivel, or the fruit to be mis-shapen.	In the future use more male blossoms per female and/or leave the female open to further pollination by bees and other insects.

Hand pollination is most successful early in the season, but after temperatures are no longer in danger of dipping below 48°F (9°C), when blossoms won't release pollen. Vines are strong enough to start setting fruit about 60 days after they were seeded. If, when you're ready to hand-pollinate, you discover that numerous fruits have already begun to set, remove the fruits to encourage the vine to produce more blossoms. Don't put off hand pollination so long that you run out of time in the growing season for fruits to mature.

Cross Pollination

All varieties within one species (*C. pepo,* for example) will readily cross with other varieties within the same species. They may also cross with other members of the gourd family, but they won't cross with all cucurbits. Pepos, for instance, won't cross with cucumbers, watermelons, or cantaloupes. No cucurbit will cross with hard-shelled gourds *(Lagenaria siceraria)* or luffa *(Luffa cylindrica).*

An interesting aspect of seed production is that each segment of the female blossom's stigma produces its own seed pocket. Since each segment may be fertilized with pollen from a different male, it's possible for each pocket to produce seeds that are genetically different from those in all other pockets. Seeds harvested from cross-pollinated vines can also grow fruit that varies in texture, taste, and tenderness from the original mother plant.

Cross-Pollination Potential

Species	Includes*	Crosses With	Rarely With
Maxima	Banana squash	moschata	argyrosperma
	Buttercup squash		pepo
	Delicious		
	Hubbard squash		
	Marrow		
	Turban		
Argyrosperma	Cushaws (except golden)	moschata	
Moschata	Butternut squash	maxima	
	Cheese	pepo	
	Melon squash		
Pepo	Acorn squash	argyrosperma	maxima
	Spaghetti squash	moschata	
	all summer squash		

Common nonpumpkins; for pumpkin varieties and species, see chart on page 20.

Since interspecies crosses don't happen readily, the average home gardener can safely plant one variety of each species. Pumpkin seed keeps well for four years or more, so you could rotate as many as four different varieties of each species, if you don't mind enjoying each only every four years. Another way to avoid cross-pollination is to separate varieties by at least 200 feet (60 m); if you're a serious seed saver, separate them by at least ¼ mile (400 m).

Pick a Peck of Pumpkins

Pumpkins must be harvested before the fall's first hard frost, which kills vines and ruins pumpkins for storage. Hard-shelled maximas can take a light frost; others must be harvested before the temperature dips below 32°F (0°C).

As harvest time approaches, pinch out plant leaders and flowers, and remove small green fruits that have no chance of ripening before frost hits. Removing immature fruit channels the vine's energy into improving the size and vigor of the remaining pumpkins. The immature fruits needn't go to waste — cook and serve them as you would summer squash.

When pumpkins reach maturity, their vines and leaves shrivel, turn brown, and die back. Fruits turn from yellow to bright orange, and rinds harden. A pumpkin isn't truly ripe for harvest until you can't readily pierce the shell with your fingernail.

Unless you're in a big hurry, leave the pumpkins on the vine until just before the season's first hard frost. They won't get overripe. Make an exception if you garden in hot, dry weather, which causes pumpkins to ripen early. If left on the vine, these pumpkins will turn soft and rot in the sun. Pumpkins in my Tennessee garden, for example, ripen and must be harvested in August; they won't wait until first frost threatens in November.

Depending on your climate, white-shelled varieties may also need to be gathered early, since they should be harvested while still streaked with green. If they are allowed to ripen fully, their shells will turn pale yellow. (Stress or disease in the vine can also cause white shells to take on a tint.) Naked seed varieties are ready to harvest when cracks appear around the stem attachment.

At the opposite end of the spectrum, in some climates pumpkins are still immature when frost threatens. Orange- or yellow-shelled varieties that are slightly streaked with green will continue to ripen after being harvested, but they won't store well, because their shells haven't naturally hardened. Early yellow varieties, developed for short-season growing, have a precocious yellow gene that causes their shells to turn yellow before darkening to orange; at harvest time these pumpkins appear ripe, even though they're still immature — but they won't keep long in storage.

Harvest pumpkins with at least 2 inches (5 cm) of stem. Don't break them from the vine, which can damage the fruit. Instead, use a sharp knife or shears to cut them off. For details on saving your harvest, see the section on curing and storing pumpkins beginning on page 189.

Saving Seeds

Saving seeds from your own pumpkins to plant another season gives you a certain sense of satisfaction. It also:

- Offers a modicum of self-sufficiency
- Gives you a hand in preserving old-time varieties
- Lets you develop pumpkins that, over time, adapt to your particular growing conditions
- Ensures that you'll have a continuing supply of seed from a variety you particularly like

Years ago I planted a Sugar pumpkin that was hardy, prolific, sweet, and extremely flavorful. In those days I hadn't yet learned to write down the names of seeds I planted and where I got them. I was so naive that I thought all Sugar pumpkins were the same. I have never again grown a pumpkin I liked quite as well. If only I had saved some seeds!

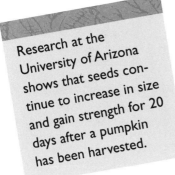

Research at the University of Arizona shows that seeds continue to increase in size and gain strength for 20 days after a pumpkin has been harvested.

If you plan to save your own seed from year to year, grow an open-pollinated variety. The seeds will produce plants similar to the parent vine,

Kid Stuff

Children love to watch their own personal pumpkins grow. When pumpkins just start turning yellow on the vine, let each child choose one and scratch his or her name or initials

into the outer skin with a nail or other pointed object. As the shell hardens, the lettering will clearly show in the form of a raised scar.

A face or other design scratched into the shell helps children learn how pumpkins stretch while they grow. To take advantage of the twisted effect that develops as the pumpkin matures, work on the design a little at a time, perhaps once a week.

A pumpkin's shape can be influenced by restricting the fruit as it grows. To make a square pumpkin, for example, grow a medium-sized variety and place each immature fruit in an empty ½-gallon cardboard milk carton. The pumpkins will develop square corners as they grow.

Caution children who work or play in the pumpkin patch that pumpkin stems are brittle and vines are hollow, so they must take great care not to break a fruit from the plant or step on a vine and crush it.

provided the flowers they came from were not inadvertently crossed with related vines growing nearby. If you prefer to grow hybrid pumpkins, you must purchase seed year after year (a major reason commercial seed sources favor hybrids). If you harvest seeds from a hybrid, they won't grow true to the parent plant, but are likely instead to either be sterile or revert to one or another of the cultivars in their genetic background.

Save seed from your best vines, and from the best fruit on those vines. Do not save seed from vines showing evidence of viral disease (mottled leaves) or anthracnose (circular sores on leaves and fruit). Harvest seed pumpkins only after they've ripened and their shells have hardened.

1. Cut open the pumpkin, scoop out its seeds, and separate as much pulp from the seeds as you can. Wash away remaining pulp by holding the seeds in a large strainer under cool running water. If the seeds have hulls, you can rub them against the strainer's wire to loosen clinging flesh; don't rub naked seeds or you might damage them.

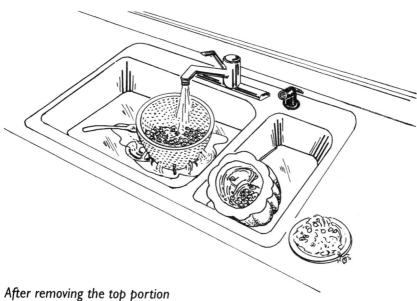

*After removing the top portion
of the pumpkin, place the pulp in a sieve
under running water to help separate out the seeds.*

2. To disinfect their surfaces, soak hulled seeds for a few minutes in a 0.5 percent solution of sodium hypochlorite (chlorine bleach mixed 2 teaspoons to the cup [10 ml/240 ml] of water); do not disinfect hull-less seeds.

3. Thoroughly dry the seeds. Spread them on screens or trays and dry them indoors, away from direct sunlight, for 10 to 14 days. Don't dry seeds in the oven — a temperature above 95°F (35°C) will damage their ability to sprout. Don't dry the seeds on paper of any sort; bits of paper may stick to them and later reabsorb moisture.

If your climate is humid, dry seeds in a large jar, along with a smaller, open jar containing silica gel of a weight equal to that of the seeds. Dry seeds are ready for storage when their moisture content is 6 to 8 percent. A seed containing the correct amount of moisture will easily break in half when you bend it; if it bends, but doesn't break, continue drying.

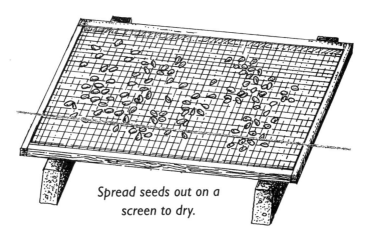

Spread seeds out on a screen to dry.

4. Before storing seeds away, sort out runts and flat seeds, which contain no embryos. Store the dried seeds in airtight containers, such as glass jars with tight-fitting lids. We keep our seeds in plastic vitamin-pill bottles stored inside an insulated picnic chest, which in turn we keep in the pantry away from light, heat, and moisture.

The best conditions under which to store seeds are humidity of less than 60 percent and temperatures of between 32 and 41°F (0°–5°C). To absorb humidity that can cause mold, include a packet of powdered milk or desiccant powder such as silica gel. Kept in airtight containers in a cool, dry place, pumpkin seeds will maintain their ability to sprout for five or six years. Each season hold back a few seeds from the season before, so you'll always be ready to make a new start in case of crop failure.

Store seeds in an insulated picnic cooler away from light, heat, and moisture.

The late Ruth Stout, who favored 'Young's Beauty' pumpkins and who promoted mulch as a time-saving method of gardening, did not save seeds indoors from year to year. Instead, she selected a fine specimen from her best vine, left it where she wanted it to grow, and covered it with hay. The next spring her volunteer pumpkins grew far faster than her neighbors' conventionally seeded crops.

We inadvertently tried Ruth's method one year, when a ripe Winter Luxury met its untimely demise under the tines of our rototiller. The next spring a volunteer vine sprouted and spread throughout the garden, and produced more prolifically than any other vine we deliberately planted that year.

Pumpkin grower Glenn Drowns saves seed from heirloom varieties including the blue 'Queensland' (foreground).

Commercial Growing

Illinois is our top pumpkin-producing state, each year supplying canneries with fruits from over 6,000 acres (2,430 ha). California comes in second, harvesting over 4,000 acres (1,620 ha). All told, according to the

International Pumpkin Association, American farmers produce some 100 million pumpkins each year.

For many farmstand growers, pumpkins are no longer a sideline but have become a major cash crop. They can be profitable, given the proper care. To get top prices for quality pumpkins requires substantial time, labor, and expense. And you have to worry about weather conditions — too much rain or prolonged heat can destroy the crop, along with the entire season's income.

Unlike growing backyard pumpkins, producing a quality, rot-free pumpkin on a commercial scale is no easy task, according to Raymond J. Samulis, Extension agent for Burlington County, New Jersey. By popular demand, Samulis holds an annual Pumpkin Grower's Meeting, at which he discusses the five main activities involved in maintaining a commercial pumpkin patch:

1. **Land preparation:** liming, plowing, disking, and planting a cover crop
2. **Planting:** purchasing seed, planting, thinning, hoeing, and applying herbicides
3. **Fertilizer:** preplant, banded, sidedressed, and supplemental foliar feeds and microelements, along with the labor of application
4. **Pest control:** fungus and insect control measures as needed to maintain fruit and stem qualities
5. **Harvest:** containers, equipment, and labor (15 man-hours per acre, 37.5 man-hours per hectare)

Commercial Practices

In many ways, growing pumpkins is similar to growing other row crops. The seedbed is usually prepared by disking and cultivating. If the soil pH is 5.6 or less, it must be sweetened with 2 tons of agricultural limestone to the acre (4.5 metric ton/ha). Sandy soil is usually deficient in boron (causing misshapen fruit) and requires the application of 1 pound of boron per acre (1 kg/ha).

Weeds may be controlled through good seedbed preparation, along with soil cultivation — mechanical cultivation until the vines spread, then hand hoeing. Many growers incorporate a preplant herbicide into the soil. Ed and Kathy Shaefer of Bellevue Berry and Pumpkin Ranch in Omaha, Nebraska, plant a cover crop. Besides controlling weeds, the cover crop residue minimizes contact between pumpkins and the soil. When the cover is tilled under, it decomposes into humus to enrich and loosen the soil.

In spring the Shaefers cover-crop their 35-acre (14.2 ha) pumpkin patch with oats or rye, which they kill or mow before it goes to seed. Then they plant 2 pounds (746 g) of compact-vining pumpkin seed, along with some ornamental corn. Pumpkins may be no-till seeded into the cover-crop residue, or seedlings may be transplanted with a bulb planter or a spade.

The salability of pumpkins often hinges on having adequate stems for handles. To ensure healthy stems, as well as fruit that's free of rot and other problems, pumpkins require an aggressive disease control program. The most important disease control measure is crop rotation. Since the Shaefers sow the same fields to pumpkins year after year, they plant

Seed Stats

Seeds per ounce (g)	approximately 200 (7)
Seeds per pound (kg)	approximately 3,000 (7,000)
Seeds per 100-foot (30 m) row	I ounce (30 g)
Seeds per acre (ha)	2–4 lbs. (1-2 kg) for a spreading vine 4–6 lbs. (2-3 kg) for a compact vine
Distance between rows	8–10 feet (2½–3 m) for a spreading vine 6–8 feet (2–2½ m) for a compact vine
Distance between plants	4–5 feet (1–2 m) for a spreading vine 2–3 feet (1 m) for a compact vine

rows through 4-foot-wide (120 cm) plastic mulch, leaving 10-foot-wide (300 cm) strips of cover between plastic strips. They take great care to move the rows each year to ensure that pumpkins aren't planted in exactly the same spot two years in a row.

Commercial growers haven't yet found a way to produce high-quality pumpkins without using fungicides heavily. Treatment begins when fruit starts to set in late July or early August. To control the spread of diseases, most growers use insecticides, applied in the evening after blossoms close, to avoid harming bees and other pollinating insects.

Recommended Nutrients for Growing Pumpkins

Nutrient	Recommended Amount	Application Method
Nitrogen (N)	50–75 lbs./acre (55–85 kg/ha)	Half broadcast and disked in prior to planting; remainder sidedressed when vines start to run
Phosphorus (P)	**Soil Test Level** low 150 lbs./acre (170 kg/ha) medium 100 lbs./acre (110 kg/ha) high 50 lbs./acre (55 kg/ha) very high 0	Broadcast and disked in prior to planting
Potassium (K)	low 200 lbs./acre (220 kg/ha) medium 150 lbs./acre (170 kg/ha) high 100 lbs./acre (110 kg/ha) very high 0	Broadcast and disked in prior to planting

Source: "Commercial Vegetable Production," Cooperative Extension Service, University of Maryland

— 4 —
The Big One

There's something about pumpkins, especially when they're big, that makes people happy. The bigger the pumpkin, the happier it seems to make them feel.

— Howard Dill
quoted in *The Pumpkin King*, by Al Kingsbury, 1992

COMPETITIVE PUMPKIN GROWING is big business, with prizes ranging as high as $10,000 and seeds from a record breaker worth as much as $10 each. A world-record pumpkin brings in several thousands of dollars more in display value. No wonder growers of giant pumpkins spend so much time studying soils, fertilizers, plant physiology, and even the effects of music on pumpkin growth.

Growing Colossal Cucurbits

Over a million people are estimated to enjoy growing giant pumpkins, the largest member of the vegetable kingdom. Producing big pumpkins is great fun, especially since you can practically see them grow — a giant approaching maturity may gain 5 inches (12 cm) of girth and 15 pounds (7 kg) or more in a single day.

Early each October, the annual pumpkin weigh-off is staged around the world. Gardeners converge on designated sites to heft their giants onto carefully calibrated scales and vie for the world record. Officials call in their site's best weights to their sponsor's headquarters, where the winner is determined. If a new record is established, it is submitted to the *Guinness Book of World Records.* To encourage the growing of exhibition pumpkins by offering prizes to its members, the Great Pumpkin Commonwealth was organized in 1993 as an informal coalition of weigh-off sites throughout the United States and Canada.

Growing giant pumpkins for sport goes back to at least the turn of the 20th century. In 1893 William Warnock of Goderich, Ontario, grew a 365-pound (166 kg) pumpkin — which in those days was considered quite a feat. In 1900 Warnock outdid his earlier effort by sending a 400-pounder (182 kg) to the Paris World's Fair. In 1903 he again topped his own record with a 403-pound (183 kg) pumpkin exhibited at the St. Louis World's Fair. Interestingly, in 1905 Warnock wrote down the basics of growing giant pumpkins, and they remain pretty much unchanged to this day.

Record-Breaking Pumpkins

Year	Entered By	Pounds
1893	William Warnock, Goderich, ON	365
1900	William Warnock, Goderich, ON	400
1903	William Warnock, Goderich, ON	403
1976	Bob Ford, Coatesville, PA	451
1980	Howard Dill, Windsor, NS	459
1981	Howard Dill, Windsor, NS	493.5
1984	Norman Gallagher, Chelan, WA	612
1986	Robert Gancarz, Wrightstown, NJ	671
1989	Gordon Thomson, Hemmingford, PQ	755
1990	Ed Gancarz, Wrightstown NJ	816.5
1992	Joel Holland, Puyallup, WA	827
1993	Donald Black, Winthrop, NY	884
1994	Herman Bax, Brockville, ON	990
1996	Nathan & Paula Zehr, Lowville, NY	1,061

The Rennie Seed Company bought a Warnock maxima — called 'Goderich Giant' after Warnock's hometown — and sold its seeds for 5 cents each. Howard Dill of Windsor, Nova Scotia, acquired some of the seeds and, through selective breeding, developed the 'Dill's Atlantic Giant' — the variety that continues to break modern-day records. The story of Howard Dill and his 'Atlantic Giant' is detailed in the book *The Pumpkin King* (listed in the appendix).

Warnock's 1903 record stood until 1976, when Bob Ford of Coatesville, Pennsylvania, entered a 451-pound (205 kg) 'Dill's Atlantic Giant' at the U.S. Pumpkin Contest in Churchville, Pennsylvania. Howard Dill beat that record in 1980 with a 459-pounder (208 kg) entered into the Cornell Contest in Pennsylvania. The following year Dill broke his own record with a 493.5-pounder (224 kg).

In 1983 Dill and fellow big-pumpkin enthusiast Ray Waterman of Collins, New York, joined forces to form the World Pumpkin

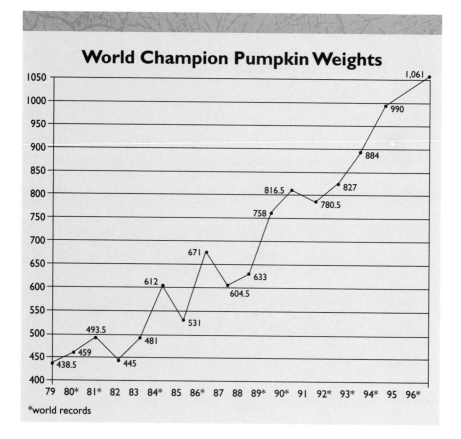

World Champion Pumpkin Weights

*world records

Confederation. At a weigh-off sponsored in 1984 by the fledgling organization, Dill's record was broken by Norman Gallagher of Chelan, Washington, who entered a 612-pound (278 kg) specimen. A 671-pound (305 kg) pumpkin grown by Robert Gancarz of Wrightstown, New Jersey, took the record in 1986, and in 1989 Gordon Thomson of Hemmingford, Quebec, won with his 755-pounder (343 kg). Since then a new world record has been established nearly every year.

People laughed when Waterman first mentioned his belief that a 1,000-pound (454 kg) pumpkin would be grown by the end of the 20th century. But when Donald Black of Winthrop, New York, entered an 884-pound (401 kg) pumpkin in 1993, no one was laughing — they were all toiling to make Waterman's "impossible" dream become a reality. The following year four growers broke the record and one of them, Herman Bax of Brockville, Ontario, established a new record just 10 pounds (4.5 kg) short of the elusive 1,000 pounds. Then, in 1996, it happened — Nathan and Paula Zehr of Lowville, New York, grew a 1,061 pound (477kg) pumpkin and Waterman was vindicated.

Ready, Set, Grow

The obvious question comes up as to why record-breaking pumpkins all come from northern states, mostly in the Northeast. One answer is that the biggest pumpkin is the cool-climate-loving maxima. The man who took it upon himself to enhance the growth rate of maximas through genetic selection happened to live in Nova Scotia, so over the years 'Dill's Atlantic Giant' pumpkins have naturally become acclimatized to northeastern conditions.

Historian Mary Joan Barrett of Mallorytown, Ontario, gleaned additional theories from competitive pumpkin growers:

- The long hot days and short cool nights of late summer in the northeastern United States and southeastern Canada are ideal for growing pumpkins, which exhibit their most spectacular growth rates from August 1 through September 15.
- Phenomenal size has something to do with the effect of growing near a large body of water, perhaps because water acts as a heat sink to create the steady climate pumpkins love. Record-breaking pumpkins have been grown near the Bay of Fundy (home of

Howard Dill), Lake Erie, Lake Huron, Boston Bay, and the St. Lawrence River.

&. A tremendous camaraderie has developed among northeastern growers, who share tips and otherwise support one another in their efforts to achieve super results.

But the fun of growing giant pumpkins needn't be confined to northern climes. In 1988 Extension agent George Killgore of Fentress County, Tennessee, launched a giant-pumpkin contest as a way to encourage more fruit and vegetable entries at his county's fair. What started out as just a little fun to spark interest in the local fair has evolved into a countywide pumpkin-growing obsession that culminates with an annual Giant Pumpkin Festival in Allardt, Tennessee, complete with a pumpkin cook-off, along with the official weigh-off.

While many gardeners would be tickled to grow a 100-to-400 pound (45–182 kg) maxima, such as the 'Big Max', the 'Big Moon', or perhaps the 'Prizewinner' — the variety for which Burpee Seeds once offered a $10,000 prize for the largest specimen over 500 pounds — competitive growers plant only 'Dill's Atlantic Giant'.

Sometimes people who see one of the big pumpkins for the first time are disappointed. It's true that these pumpkins are huge, but their shells look pale and washed out compared to the bright orange color you'd expect of a proper pumpkin. Worse, the shape is somewhat flattened, as if the old boy had grown tired of the whole thing and was about to give up. Still, in size alone these big fellows are impressive enough.

As you might expect, prima donna pumpkins need plenty of pampering. Contradictory advice abounds, leading to the conclusion that the only road to success is to find the right combination of techniques for your unique growing conditions. That's what makes growing the Big One such a challenge.

Today all record-breaking pumpkins are grown from 'Dill's Atlantic Giant' seed.

To start you in the right direction, you'll find a wealth of information in newsletters put out by organizations such as the New England Pumpkin Growers Association and the Atlantic Pumpkin Growers' Association. If you're truly serious about competitive growing, read *How to Grow World-Class Giant Pumpkins* by Don Langevin. These and other resources are listed in the appendix.

Pumpkinology 101

Growing a pumpkin in the competition category takes 120 days or more. The vine uses the first half of its life to develop a support system in preparation for flowering and pollination. The second half of the vine's life is devoted to fruit development and growth.

Site Preparation

For competitive growers, gardening starts in autumn. Select a sunny spot, since your vine will need all-day sunlight for maximum growth. On the chosen spot, heap leaves and manure, effectively creating a small compost pile. By planting time, the following mid-May to mid-June (depending on your last frost date), the leaves and manure should be well rotted, providing a fertile bed for your pumpkin vine.

The next spring, prepare the seedbed by digging the rotted manure into the soil in a 30-foot (9 m) circle. At the center of the circle prepare a hill 8 to 10 feet (2.4–3 m) in diameter, 12 inches (30 cm) high at center, and gradually tapering to ground level around the edges.

If you're growing more than one Atlantic Giant, space the hills 50 feet (15 m) apart — or 20 feet (6 m) apart for lesser maximas — to give vines plenty of room to grow. Each vine will take up at least 1,000 square feet (90 sq. m) and may cover as much as 2,000 square feet (180 sq. m). Plant four seeds in the center of each hill. When the seedlings have four to six true leaves, pinch off all but the single best plant.

Because 'Dill's Atlantic Giant' seeds are more difficult to sprout than those of other pumpkins, most serious growers start their seeds indoors or in a cold frame and move them outside when the soil is sufficiently warm. Herman Bax started the seed that grew his 990-pound (449 kg) pumpkin by first sanding the edges of the seed, soaking it for a few hours in a liquid fertilizer solution, then presprouting it (as described on page 49). To avoid losing valuable growing time due to germination difficulties, Hugh Wiberg of Wilmington, Massachusetts, suggests asking a local nursery to sprout your seeds, which it may do for a small fee. Until the weather becomes consistently warm, cover seeds and seedlings with a plastic tent or hot cap to keep the soil warm and moist.

Most record-breaking pumpkins are grown in nearly neutral soil (pH near 7.0). The soil in Howard Dill's Nova Scotia garden is acidic and requires constant additions of calcium in the form of dolomitic limestone or agricultural gypsum. Gypsum, says Dill, has an advantage over limestone in that it frees up more nutrients, breaks up heavy, wet soils and reduces the risk of fruit rot and splitting. A less expensive source of calcium is crushed eggshells, liberally worked into the soil at planting time.

Wind Protection

Even after the weather warms, continue to protect your seedlings from wind, which can dry them out and seriously set them back. Wind can be a big problem for the stem of a young giant still in the upright stage, before it flops over and begins sending out runners. A strong wind can snap it right in two.

As your giant grows it will develop giant leaves, perhaps more than 2 feet (60 cm) across. These leaves act as sails that catch wind, sometimes ripping a vine out by its roots. A heavy wind may even roll a big pumpkin, causing it to rip out roots and crush the vine.

Many growers construct a small plastic cold frame that does double duty by both protecting a seedling from wind and keeping it warm.

A miniature cold frame keeps seedlings warm and protects them from wind.

When the vine outgrows its house, use crossed stakes to anchor runners and keep wind from whipping them around. One foot (30 cm) from the end of each runner, place one stake on each side of the vine, then cross the two stakes to keep the vine in contact with soil, which encourages rooting. But take great care not to crush the hollow vine. As roots develop and runners grow, move the stakes to a new spot closer to the tip.

Crossed stakes prevent runners from blowing in the wind.

Encouraging Root Growth

The more roots a vine has, the better it's anchored to the ground, and the less susceptible it is to wind damage. An extensive root system also brings more moisture and nutrients to the fruit, ensuring maximum growth. And if the vine is attacked by borer (described on page 102), the more roots it has, the more likely the plant is to survive.

A vine will develop roots anywhere that a leaf stem grows. Encourage rooting by burying every leaf node that appears on the vine. Between runners, put down boards to provide pathways for tending your vine, so your footsteps won't compact the soil and inhibit penetration by new roots.

After about three or four weeks, a vine's roots range widely. To avoid damaging them, don't hoe weeds: Carefully pull them out by hand. A liberal layer of mulch also works wonders in keeping weeds at bay. The vine's own network of large leaves will eventually shade the soil, keeping down weeds and holding in moisture.

The one place you don't want roots to grow is in the vicinity of your established pumpkin. As the pumpkin grows, it may pull nearby roots out of the ground. On the other hand, if the roots are strong enough to hold fast, the pumpkin may instead pull itself off the vine. Keep your pumpkin from breaking off at the stem by discouraging the vine from putting down nearby roots. Either slip a sheet of plastic under the vine, or every few days run your hand along the bottom of the vine, breaking off any anchor roots that try to form within 3 feet (1 m) on each side of the growing fruit.

Watering Your Giants

Giants grow best in soil that remains moist, but not wet, to a depth of at least 6 inches (15 cm). Howard Dill estimates that each vine needs 40 to 50 gallons (150–190 L) of water a week. In dry weather, some growers apply as much as 300 gallons (1,140 L) every two to three days.

Water as often as necessary to keep the soil evenly moist. Deep, but less frequent, watering is better than daily watering; too frequent watering can cause the fruit to split, especially in heavy soil. Depending on your soil type, you may need to water either once or twice a week.

Since a giant vine has a large root system, liberally water the soil along the entire vine, not just near the main root. Apply water only to the soil — never to leaves or fruit — to avoid sun scald and to minimize the risk of spreading bacteria and fungi.

Feeding Your Giants

Like all large living things, giant pumpkins eat a lot. Start your transplanted seedlings by feeding them 1 gallon (4 L) of liquid fertilizer solution or compost tea (described on page 96). Repeat one week later with another gallon. Continue applying fertilizer and water in copious quantities throughout the growing season.

Most of the vine's growth will occur during its first 60 to 70 days, from the appearance of true leaves until the occurrence of fruit set. During that time, a vine may stretch as much as 1 foot (30 cm) each day. In its early stages of growth, the vine needs plenty of phosphorus for root development. Later its nutrient needs shift toward nitrogen for green leaves, then to potassium (potash) for good fruit set. Potassium supplies are usually sufficient in the soil, particularly soil containing plenty of well-rotted manure.

As fruit set approaches, usually in early July, a foolproof way to see that your vine gets plenty of nutrients is to apply a 4-inch (10 cm) layer of rotted manure in a wide circle around the main stem. Some growers swear by horse manure, others won't use anything but chicken manure. The "best" manure is what's on hand, as long as it's well aged to avoid burning your vine with hot fresh nitrogen.

Many growers prefer to spray on foliar nutrients twice weekly, applying the spray at five times the normal rate (or using fish emulsion

Nutrient Needs

Nutrient	Purpose
Blood meal or fish meal	Green leaves and vines
Bone meal or rock phosphate	Flower and root development Disease resistance
Kelp meal or greensand	Fruit set Thick, sweet fruit

combined with an equal amount of water). Vines should be sprayed in early morning, before the dew dries. Foliar nutrient sprays are especially useful when the air is extremely humid. High humidity reduces the evaporation rate of moisture from leaves, causing roots to absorb less water and therefore fewer nutrients.

In areas of high rainfall, though, or where vines are watered with overhead sprinklers, no more than 10 percent of foliar feed enters a plant through its leaves, according to Wayne Hackney of New Milford, Connecticut, who publishes an informative beginner's handout (listed in the appendix). The rest gets washed off into the soil and is absorbed by the vine's roots. In such cases, why spend time frequently spraying leaves, when a liberal application of compost or well-rotted manure will accomplish the same thing?

Setting Fruit

Even without foliar feeding, a pumpkin vine obtains nutrients through its leaves by using sunlight for photosynthesis. Expert growers estimate that each leaf can sustain up to 4 pounds (1.8 kg) of fruit. Since it takes a *big* vine to grow a *big* pumpkin, don't let your plant set fruit until it has at least 300 leaves, approximately in midsummer when runners are about 10 feet (3 m) long.

Until your vine is of adequate size to bear fruit, remove any female blossoms or baby pumpkins that appear. When you judge the vine to be big enough, with enough leaves, continue removing all but the ideal blossoms. To ensure that the Big One grows exactly where you want it, hand-pollinate (as described beginning on page 61) your best blossoms instead of letting nature take its course. An ideal blossom to pollinate has these four characteristics:

1. It grows on a main vine, not on a secondary runner, to ensure that it gets plenty of nutrients.

2. It grows no closer than 10 feet (3 m) from the main stem, to keep it from ripping out the main root as it grows.

The ideal blossom has a stigma with five or more segments, each of which will become a seed pocket.

3. Its stem grows at a 90-degree angle from the vine, so the pumpkin's shoulder won't push against the vine.

4. Its stigma is made up of four or five segments. (The more normal the blossom, the more uniformly the fruit will grow.)

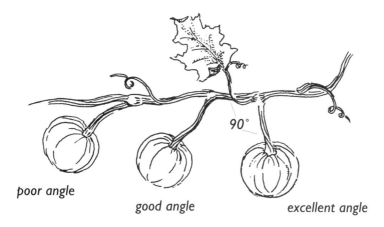

poor angle

good angle

excellent angle

90°

Competitive growers disagree on how many pumpkins to grow on each vine. Serious contenders allow only one fruit per plant to reach maturity. Many growers initially set one fruit on each main runner, since baby giants have the nasty habit of aborting in their early stages of growth. You can readily identify a fruit that's about to abort — it will be slow growing and dull looking. A shiny yellow fruit, on the other hand, is probably healthy.

Once you've selected your ideal specimens, remove any other fruits that develop. You want all the vine's nutrients to go into growing the pumpkins of your choice. When the pumpkins reach approximately volleyball size, cut off all but the best one or two.

Some growers place a square of plywood, Styrofoam, or corrugated plastic (poked with holes for drainage) or a bed of straw or sand beneath

Barb Hubbard of Kentville, NS, shows how much her pumpkin grew between August 3 and September 22 — just 50 days.

each pumpkin to protect the bottom from insects and moisture, both of which can cause rot. Other growers don't bother and don't have any trouble. Whether or not you protect your pumpkin with a platform, from this point on don't move or turn it, or you'll run the risk of breaking its stem.

Check your vine every five days or so, searching out and removing any newly forming fruit that would otherwise rob nutrients from your potential prizewinner. Bury the tips of new growth to encourage auxiliary roots that will help feed the little monster. Your pumpkin should put on no less than 2 inches (5 cm) and 5 pounds (2.25 kg) a day throughout August and September. Herman Bax's winning 990-pounder gained 94 pounds (42 kg) in just three days. Every 10 days, feed your Goliath a shot of manure tea or other liquid fertilizer.

Other tips offered by distinguished pumpkin experts:

- Guard vigilantly against diseases and insects (the subject of the next chapter).
- Keep your pumpkins happy by playing music to them.
- Never let your vines become stressed due to lack of water, shortage of nutrients, or excessive heat.

Avoiding Heat Stress

One of the secrets of pumpkin-growing success is to avoid stressing your leviathan, and one of the most difficult kinds of stress to avoid is heat stress, which occurs when temperatures soar above 90°F (32°C). Hot sun combined with low humidity causes moisture to evaporate from leaves faster than the roots can absorb more. The result is dehydration, which toughens a pumpkin's shell prematurely; as the pumpkin continues to grow, the shell will crack. Your vine is experiencing heat stress when its leaves wilt and scorch.

Vines are less likely to be stressed when grown in soil with a good water-retention capacity. Large amounts of humus (compost) or vermiculite, worked into the soil to a depth of at least 18 inches (45 cm), improve the soil's ability to hold moisture. A phosphorus-rich fertilizer promotes a large root structure, which increases the vine's ability to absorb water during times of stress.

Protect your Baby Huey from the sun by erecting four posts and a roof, raised a couple of feet over the pumpkin, or by gently arranging vines and large leaves over your pumpkin to provide some shade. Interestingly, the characteristic pale color of 'Atlantic Giant' is its own defense against sun scald and heat stress.

A simple shelter constructed of four posts and a roof will protect your giant pumpkin from hot sun.

Pruning

Your giant pumpkin vine will need pruning for two reasons:

- A controlled vine is easier to manage than a large, sprawly vine, and therefore is more likely to get the care it needs to remain healthy.
- The larger your gonzo pumpkin gets, the more you need to divert nutrients from the leaves to the fruit.

A good plant size, says expert Howard Dill, is 20 to 25 feet (6–7.5 m) in diameter. When your vine reaches that size, likely by late August, start pinching off the tips of all runners. In early September, cut off new side runners before they set down roots. Continue removing new growth until your pumpkin is ready for harvest and snip off any baby pumpkins that appear.

Throughout the season, train vines to grow away from your pumpkin's shoulders so the fruit can expand without pushing against the vine or crushing a runner. Howard Dill nudges his vines daily.

Howard Dill has broken the world record four times.

Big Challenges

The two biggest challenges for growers of giant pumpkins are to prevent splitting and to successfully transport the pumpkin to the competition site.

Splitting

Even the most experienced growers scratch their heads over how to prevent splitting. Tiny cracks can usually be dealt with, but the party is over if your pumpkin is a victim of "blow out" — meaning it grows so fast that it literally bursts.

You already know two ways to prevent splitting: Keep anchor roots from growing within 3 feet (1 m) of either side of your pumpkin, so the expanding fruit won't split at the stem and break off the vine; and protect your pumpkin from hot sun, which can reduce the shell's pliability and ability to stretch as the pumpkin grows.

Small cracks that appear in the shell may heal on their own, but will benefit from your assistance. Moisture that gets into a crack invites bacteria and fungi, ultimately leading to rot and the collapse of your season's efforts. Once rot sets in, the offending pumpkin must be removed so its disease won't spread to others.

Tree-grafting wax, applied to surface cracks, will seal out moisture. Spraying the pumpkin weekly with a solution of chlorine bleach (3 tablespoons of bleach per quart [47 ml/L] of water) will discourage bacteria. A weekly application of fungicide will deter fungi. (For more information on disease control, see chapter 5.)

A pumpkin that cracks under its own weight may be a casualty of improper watering or feeding. If you let the soil dry out around your vine and then water liberally, the roots will eagerly soak up moisture and carry it to the fruit, which will swell and split. Keep the soil evenly moist to a depth of at least 6 inches (15 cm). Lavish applications of chemical fertilizers supply nutrients in periodic bursts, leading to growth surges that also cause splitting. For balanced growth, either apply chemicals in small, steady doses or feed your pumpkin through the use of plenty of rotted manure or compost, which supply a steady stream of nutrients.

If, despite all your precautions, your pumpkin splits anyway, chalk it up to bad luck and try again next year. The likelihood that a pumpkin will split is one reason many growers hedge their bets by tending more than one vine each season. Even if your best pumpkin falls victim to blowout, who knows — your next best pumpkin might still be big enough to set a new world record.

Transporting

Nothing can make a grown man cry like believing he has the prize sewn up, then seeing his pride and joy burst open due to mishandling during transport. Over the years, as pumpkins have gotten heavier, moving them has gotten trickier. The secret is to always handle the pumpkin gently. Never jar, drop, or plunk it down, or you run the risk of popping it wide open.

To move a lesser giant, a wheelbarrow and a few friends are all you need. Pad the barrow with an old blanket, or other soft lining, and tilt it on its side next to the pumpkin. While some helpers hold the wheelbarrow steady, others roll the pumpkin in, then all hands help tilt the barrow upright while keeping the pumpkin from rolling out.

A smaller maxima can also be moved with a heavy blanket, piece of carpet, or canvas tarp. But for a pumpkin weighing 400 pounds (182 kg) or more, use nothing less than a reinforced tarp with handles. Howard Dill has designed a pumpkin-moving tarp, which he makes available to growers. You can find other sources through weigh-off officials or pumpkin growers' organizations (some are listed at the back of this book).

With the help of several friends, carefully roll your pumpkin onto its edge (remember, it has a flat bottom), lay down the tarp, and carefully

Pad a wheelbarrow with an old blanket and tilt it on its side to roll the pumpkin in. You may need a few helpers to tilt the wheelbarrow back up.

lower the pumpkin back down onto the tarp. Have at least eight strong helpers on hand to lift the pumpkin-laden tarp.

Of course, you could always use a forklift, but you'll still need a passel of friends to lift the tarp onto a well-padded pallet. Anchor the pumpkin to the pallet with straps, so the fruit of your labors won't get jostled off.

Whatever method you choose for moving your ponderous pumpkin, expect it to lose at least 5 pounds (2 kg) per day in transit.

Estimating Weight

Howard Dill and his friend Leonard Stellpflug of Rush, New York, have developed a chart for estimating the weight of a pumpkin based on its measurements. The key word here is *estimating,* cautions Howard's son Danny, who follows closely in his father's footsteps. A giant pumpkin's flesh can vary from 3 to 8 inches (7.5–20 cm) thick, throwing estimates off by as much as 100 pounds (45 kg).

Since looks can be deceiving, your biggest pumpkin won't necessarily be your heaviest. Wayne Hackney tells of a friend who took his largest pumpkin to the fair, leaving a smaller one behind. The larger pumpkin, by measurements, had an estimated weight of 580 pounds (263 kg). The smaller one, the fellow later determined, weighed 641 pounds (291 kg) — enough to have won the competition.

To estimate your pumpkin's weight by measuring its size:

I. Measure the *largest* circumference, parallel to the ground at approximately stem to blossom level.

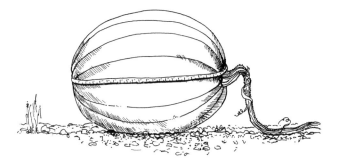

Pricing Your Prizewinner

The more a pumpkin weighs, the more it's worth per pound. The New England Pumpkin Growers Association suggests a starting price of 25 cents per pound, going up 5 cents for each 100 pounds (45 kg). That makes a 90-pound (41 kg) pumpkin worth 25 cents per pound, while a 105-pounder (48 kg) would bring 30 cents per pound, and a 220-pounder (100 kg) would be 35 cents per pound. Since these are suggested minimums, a pumpkin with excellent shape and color could bring more. Of course, if your pumpkin qualifies for *Guinness,* the sky's the limit. In 1994 Herman Bax sold his 990-pound record breaker for $10.50 per pound, or a total of $10,400.

2. Measure over the top at the *widest* distance (or *highest,* whichever is greater), from ground level on one side to ground level on the other side. Don't follow the fruit's contour to the ground, but take this measurement *straight down* from the widest edges of the fruit.

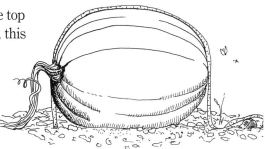

3. Again measure over the top from ground to ground, this time from stem end to blossom end at the highest point.

4. Add these three measurements together and find the estimated weight on the accompanying chart.

Estimating the Weight of Your Big Pumpkin

Inches	Lbs.	Centimeters	Inches	Lbs.	Centimeters
142	69	355	206	193	515
144	72	360	208	198	520
146	75	365	210	204	525
148	78	370	212	209	530
150	81	375	214	215	535
152	84	380	216	220	540
154	87	385	218	226	454
156	90	390	220	232	550
158	93	395	222	238	555
160	96	400	224	244	560
162	99	205	226	250	565
164	102	410	228	256	570
166	106	415	230	262	575
168	110	420	232	269	580
170	114	425	234	275	585
172	118	430	236	282	590
174	121	435	238	288	595
176	125	440	240	295	600
178	129	445	242	302	605
180	133	450	244	309	610
182	137	455	246	316	615
184	141	460	248	323	620
186	146	465	250	330	625
188	150	470	252	337	630
190	155	475	254	345	635
192	159	480	256	352	640
194	164	485	258	360	645
196	169	490	260	368	650
198	173	495	262	376	655
200	178	500	264	384	660
202	183	505	266	392	665
204	188	510	268	400	670

Inches	Lbs.	Centimeters	Inches	Lbs.	Centimeters
270	408	675	336	746	840
272	417	680	338	759	845
274	425	685	340	771	850
276	434	690	342	784	855
278	442	695	344	797	860
280	451	700	346	810	865
282	460	705	348	823	870
284	469	710	350	836	875
286	479	715	352	849	880
288	488	720	354	862	885
290	497	725	356	875	890
292	507	730	358	889	895
294	516	735	360	903	900
296	526	740	362	912	905
298	536	745	364	931	910
300	546	750	366	945	915
302	556	755	368	960	920
304	566	760	370	974	925
306	576	765	372	989	930
308	587	770	374	1003	935
310	598	775	376	1018	940
312	600	780	378	1033	945
314	619	785	380	1048	950
316	630	790	382	1063	955
318	641	795	384	1079	960
320	652	800	386	1095	965
322	664	805	388	1111	970
324	675	810	390	1127	975
326	687	815	392	1143	980
328	698	820	394	1159	985
330	710	825	396	1175	990
332	722	830	398	1191	995
334	734	835	400	1208	1000

– 5 –
Pumpkin Pests

*Y*ou need good seed, good soil, good weather, and good luck.

— Gordon Thomson
quoted in *How to Grow World-Class
Giant Pumpkins*, by Don Langevin, 1993

WHETHER YOU GROW PUMPKINS for food, fun, or fair-going, the fruits of your labors are vulnerable to attack by a myriad of insects and diseases. Which pests are most likely to bother your vines depends on where you live and on the way you garden.

Problem Solvers

If you grow healthy vines in fertile, humus-rich soil, they are less likely to be attacked by diseases and pests. So your first line of defense is to work plenty of compost or rotted barnyard manure into the soil of your pumpkin patch.

Even the healthiest plant may develop problems during times of stress, however, such as when fruits start to set or when the season brings drought, high heat, or constant rain. A stressed plant is more likely to be attacked by insects or diseases, which cause the plant more stress and attract yet more insects and diseases.

Resistant cultivars may be available that are less susceptible than others to pests or diseases prevalent in your area. Genes that confer resistance are being discovered every day. Researchers at Cornell University, among others, are actively seeking such genetic solutions to pumpkin problems.

Some heritage varieties naturally contain one or more resistant genes, which are isolated and genetically bred into many newer varieties. When you select seeds from a catalog, look for initials such as BW for "bacterial wilt," and CMV, for "cucumber mosaic virus," which indicate resistance. The vine may still be somewhat susceptible, but not as much as one without the resistance gene.

Floating row covers (such as Reemay) protect seedlings and young plants from insects that cause damage and transmit diseases. As fringe benefits, floating covers trap and retain heat, as well as offering protection from wind. Check vines to make sure no insects are present before you apply the floating cover. Anchor the cover well all around, so pests can't slip in at the edges. As soon as female blossoms appear, either remove the cover so bees and other beneficial insects can pollinate, or be prepared to hand-pollinate.

Sticky traps will capture flying insects. Purchase traps ready-made or make your own using Tanglefoot, Tangle-Trap (available from many seed and nursery catalogs), motor oil, or petroleum jelly. Spread this sticky stuff on squares of cardboard, painted bright yellow, or in yellow plastic bowls (such as those in which margarine is sold), to imitate a pumpkin blossom. Hang the trap among your vines and insects will get stuck when they come to investigate.

Handpicking insect pests, their eggs, and their larvae makes sense only if you have a few pampered pumpkin vines. A problem with handpicking is that you have to keep at it, and in doing so you run the risk of stepping on and crushing your vines. Another problem is what to do with the pests once you have them in hand. The fastest way to get rid of them is to drop them into a can of kerosene.

Water, applied to vines in a hard spray, dislodges small insects such as aphids and spider mites. To avoid encouraging fungal diseases, spray vines only in the morning, so the leaves have time to dry out before nightfall. Water helps prevent diseases in another way — keeping your vines properly watered keeps them from becoming stressed.

Soap, added to water, kills soft-bodied insects such as aphids and spider mites. Stir 1 teaspoon of nondetergent soap into 1 quart of water (5 ml/L) and test the mixture on a few leaves to make sure the kind of soap you use won't burn pumpkin leaves. If they haven't burned by the next day, go ahead and spray infested leaves. The spray must land on insects to kill them.

Soap also acts as a surfactant to spread other ingredients and help them stick. Barbara Pleasant, author of *The Gardener's Bug Book,* offers this all-purpose pest control formula: Whirl in a blender until liquefied 4 to 6 cloves of garlic, 1 small pungent onion, 2 hot peppers (or 1 teaspoon [5 ml] of ground cayenne pepper), and 1 quart (1 L) of water. Set the mixture aside overnight, then strain. Add 3 drops of liquid soap and apply the mixture with a pump sprayer.

Compost tea, used to water seedlings, helps alleviate transplant shock. When compost tea is sprayed on pumpkin vines, the bacteria in it suppress fungal diseases such as downy mildew and powdery mildew. I keep a constant supply of compost tea in a 5-gallon bucket, but you can use something smaller (such as a milk jug) or larger (such as a covered trash container). Since this tea may not smell so great, place your container where the odor won't offend anyone.

Fill one-third of your container with finished compost consisting largely of barnyard manure, and top it off with plain water. Set the container in the shade for three or four days, during which the brew will ferment. Stir occasionally. When new froth no longer appears on top, strain out larger particles (I use an old kitchen strainer) and spread the solids as fertilizer around the bases of vines.

Using a hose-attachment set to dilute the tea with equal parts of water, thoroughly soak your vines, coating both sides of leaves. To keep damp leaves from being burned by the sun, spray vines in the early morning. Respray every two weeks.

Diatomaceous earth is a form of silica derived from the skeletal remains of algae in the Bacillariophyceae class. When ground up into a powder, its pieces have sharp edges that slice into soft-bodied plant pests, causing dehydration and death. Diatomaceous earth softens when wet, so it must be reapplied after a rain or heavy watering. The washed-away diatomaceous earth isn't lost, though — it dissolves to supply pumpkin vines with several important mineral nutrients.

Create a favorable environment and beneficial creatures will be attracted to your pumpkin patch.

Beneficial creatures prey on insects that attack pumpkin vines. Some occur naturally in the environment. Birds are attracted to a garden by nearby hedgerows and trees that offer safe hiding places, and ornamental berry bushes on which they feed. Ladybugs and other beneficial insects may be attracted by a variety of herbs and flowers on which they feed, including butterfly weed, cosmos, daisy, dill, fennel, marigold, nasturtium, tansy, and zinnia.

Some beneficials (such as ladybugs, parasitic and predatory wasps, and beneficial nematodes) may be purchased and imported into your pumpkin patch. I have found, though, that purchased insects won't stay around unless the conditions are just right, and if conditions are favorable you'll attract plenty of beneficials without spending a dollar. I would consider buying beneficials only to resolve a serious infestation. Mail-order sources put out catalogs that tell you exactly which species of beneficials attack which bad bugs, and how to introduce them into your garden. (A source of a current list of suppliers appears in the appendix.)

Chemical sprays often kill good bugs as well as bad ones. Furthermore, once you start a program of chemical control, you'll likely have to continue it on a regular basis, with repeats whenever the dust or spray is washed off by rain. If you plan only to display your pumpkins, and not to eat them, you can reduce the number of applications by using a systemic product that absorbs through the roots and permeates all parts of the plant, including the fruit. You'll have to keep up with the latest information on what works, what's currently available, and what's been banned. (The latest information on chemical control for pumpkins appears in the annual report "Commercial Vegetable Production," listed in the appendix.)

Commercial growers and serious giant-pumpkin competitors are most likely to rely on chemical insecticides. A pumpkin on public display, however, is often touched by admirers, many of them children. So if you use agricultural sprays, take it easy toward harvest time. Carefully read and follow all instructions. Wear a respirator while applying poisons. Avoid touching or breathing sprays and dusts, even those derived from natural products. If you get any on yourself, wash your skin. Spray or dust only infested vines. Protect honeybees by covering treated vines with floating row covers or old sheets for a week following spraying or dusting.

If you find you need chemical means of disease and pest control, the following so-called "natural" products degrade rapidly and therefore pose the least damage to the environment:

- *Bordeaux* is a mixture of copper, lime, and sulfur that controls the less persistent bacterial and fungal diseases by penetrating leaves to kill early disease spores. It can, however, damage young vines, especially at temperatures above 80°F (27°C). Use bordeaux only as a last resort.

- *Neem* is a stomach poison that kills insects as they feed. It minimally harms beneficials, and may (the jury is still out on this) work as a fungicide. Otherwise known as azadirachtin, it's more commonly called neem because it comes from the seed of the tropical neem tree. "Align" is registered for use on edible crops grown outdoors.

- *Pyrethrin,* derived from pyrethrum daisies, is a fast-acting contact poison that kills chewing and sucking insects. Pyrethroids are artificial pyrethrins and are much more toxic, so don't get the two confused.

- *Bacillus thuringiensis* (Bt) is a bacterium that attacks insects in the larval stage. Although it's nontoxic to animals and humans, it does kill beneficial butterfly larvae and it can cause resistant strains of harmful insects to develop, so use it sparingly. Bt comes in various forms — powdered, granular, and liquid. I prefer the powder, which I put into an old nylon stocking; I can then lightly coat leaves by bouncing the stocking as I carry it over affected vines. Different strains of Bt attack different insects, so read the label to be sure you're getting the kind you need.

Solarizing the soil may be helpful in controlling pumpkin-vine attackers that live on or near the soil's surface. The chief problem with soil solarization is that it requires sunshine and a temperature of at least 85°F (29°C) for four weeks, which in many climates does not occur before pumpkins must be planted. If you have a serious problem, however, you might try solarizing the soil late in the season, in preparation for the next spring's planting.

Cultivate the soil, apply a thick layer of fresh manure, shape your growing hills, water the soil, and let it settle overnight. The next day, lay a soaker hose over the hill, cover the hill with clear construction plastic, and shovel soil all around the edges to anchor the plastic so no air can escape. Allow the sun to heat the soil through the plastic for at least four weeks. The sustained high temperature under the plastic will kill bacteria and fungi in the top 4 inches (10 cm) of soil. Without lifting the plastic, resoak the soil once during the solarization. At the end of four weeks, you may pull out the soaker hose, but leave the plastic in place until you're ready to plant (it will help warm the soil the next spring). When you ultimately remove the plastic, in preparation for sowing seed or transplanting seedlings, water the hill but don't cultivate the soil, which should be disturbed as little as possible.

Control weeds in and around your pumpkin patch, since weeds harbor insects and sometimes diseases. If you grow only a few vines, mulch to discourage weed growth. Most large-scale growers use herbicides to control grass and weeds after runners start to spread, since controlling weeds through cultivation at that point requires great care, to avoid injuring a vine's shallow roots.

Crop rotation is the most important measure you can take to control diseases and pests, many of which are harbored in the soil and are particular about the kinds of plants they attack. Rotating pumpkins with cover crops or nonrelated vegetable crops breaks the cycle. Do not incorporate into your rotation any vegetables that are subject to the same diseases as pumpkins, including other cucurbits (melons, cucumbers, or squash), as well as eggplant, lettuce, peppers, spinach, and tomatoes. The best crops to plant prior to pumpkins are legumes (beans, peas, clover, etc.); the second best are cabbage and other leafy green crops.

Bad Bugs

Which insect pests are most likely to attack your pumpkin vines depends on where in the country you garden. In nearly all locations the chief pests are the vine borer, squash bug, and cucumber beetle, but several lesser evils also lurk in the pumpkin patch.

Aphids

Aphids, sometimes called plant lice, include hundreds of winged and wingless species in the family Aphididae. These tiny creatures, found throughout the United States, are only about 1/10 inch (2.5 mm) long. They come in a variety of colors, including green, gray, black, and brown. They are extremely prolific, and are most active during periods of hot weather. Their biggest threat to pumpkin vines is their ability to spread the viral disease mosaic.

Aphids feed in large colonies, sucking moisture from stems, blossoms, and leaves and causing leaves to curl and pucker. They are often found on tender shoots or the undersides of leaves, especially of plants grown with too much nitrogen or too little humus. These relatively inactive insects put out a sticky substance called honeydew that attracts ants, so if you see ants trailing along your vines, look for aphid colonies.

To *avoid* aphids:

- Cover plants with floating row covers until female blossoms appear.
- Mulch with sheets of aluminum foil or transparent or opaque plastic. The aluminum or plastic confuses aphids about where to land.
- Remove weed and garden debris at season's end.
- Cultivate the soil twice in fall and twice again in spring.

Pumpkin Pests

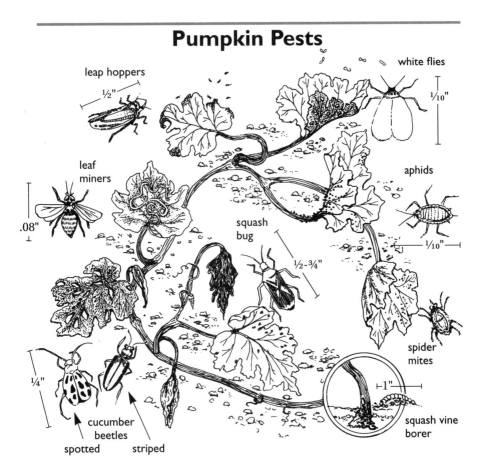

leap hoppers
½"

white flies
1/10"

leaf miners
.08"

aphids
1/10"

squash bug
½–¾"

spider mites

cucumber beetles
spotted   striped
¼"

squash vine borer
1"

You can identify pumpkin pests by "reading" the damage they do to leaves.

To *control* aphids:

- Knock them off with a strong spray of water from the hose.
- Hang sticky traps.
- Spray soapy water, insecticidal soap, or neem directly on them.
- If all else fails, apply pyrethrins or rotenone.

Natural enemies: aphid midges, daddy longlegs, green lacewings, ladybugs, parasitic wasps.

Borers

The borer, also known as the pickleworm *(Diaphania nitidalis)*, is found primarily in the Southeast, but sometimes as far north as New York and as far west as Nebraska. This ¾-inch (19 mm) grub is yellowish white with dark spots when young, turning greenish with a brown head as it matures.

As a caterpillar it may enter a bud or tunnel through fruit, and sometimes goes from one pumpkin to another. The pupa hibernates in a rolled leaf, from which it emerges in late spring. The adult is a yellow or tan moth that lays one or more eggs on nearly any part of a vine.

To *avoid* borers:

- Grow summer squash nearby to lure borers away from pumpkin vines.
- Prop pumpkins off the ground to keep borers from entering the fruit.

To *control* borers:

- Crush rolled leaves to destroy the pupae inside.
- If you find chewed blossoms, spray vines with BtK, a Bt strain.
- Remove and destroy damaged fruit.

Cucumber Beetles

The cucumber beetle, often called the squash beetle, is about ¼ inch (6 mm) long; it may be yellow or pale orange with black stripes *(Acalymma vittata)* or spots *(Diabrotica undecimpunctata howardi)*. Both species are found primarily in eastern North America, where they produce one or two generations up North, and as many as four generations down South. The striped beetle is more likely to invade pumpkin vines than the spotted.

Adults feed on stems and leaves, causing the latter to turn yellow. Except when they attack seedlings (which they can defoliate in a matter of hours), they don't seriously damage the vine, but they can blemish a pumpkin shell. Worse, while moving from plant to plant they spread bacterial wilt and mosaic virus. An infested pumpkin patch may therefore fail to bear fruit.

Feeding adults lay eggs in the soil beneath the vines. Within two weeks the eggs hatch and the larvae, called rindworms, begin tunneling through plant roots. Larvae of the striped beetle are ⅓ inch (8 mm) long and white. Larvae of the spotted beetle are ½ inch (12 mm) long and beige, with a darker head and a spot on the last body segment. The larvae overwinter in the soil, where they feed on root residue; adults overwinter in plant debris.

To *avoid* cucumber beetles:

- Cultivate in early spring to expose rindworms to natural predators.
- Avoid planting pumpkins near cucumbers.
- Seed radishes just before or at the same time as pumpkins, so they'll flower at about the same time.
- Grow pumpkin cultivars known to tolerate cucumber beetles, bacterial wilt, and mosaic virus.
- Spread diatomaceous earth around the bases of seedlings to destroy emerging larvae.
- Protect seedlings from feeding adults by covering them with floating row covers.
- Burn old vines at the end of each season.

To *control* cucumber beetles if your pumpkin patch experienced a serious infestation the previous year:

- Don't plant pumpkins (or other cucurbits) in the same soil two years in a row.
- In the South (where cucumber beetles are the adult version of southern corn rootworms), don't plant pumpkins with corn, and don't rotate pumpkins after corn.
- Control larvae by drenching soil weekly with parasitic nematodes.
- Keep early beetles from reproducing by trapping them in saucers of water topped with a thin layer of oil.
- If all else fails, apply pyrethrins, rotenone, or sabadilla in the early morning, before the beetles become active; cover the treated vines for three days with sheets or floating row covers, so the beetles can't escape the poison.

Natural enemies: beneficial nematodes, soldier beetles, spotted chalcid wasps, striped tachinid fly *(Celatoria diabrotica)*.

Cutworms

Cutworms are the soft-bodied, hairless caterpillars of various gray or brown moths in the Noctuidae family, found throughout North America. Depending on the prevalent species, they may produce one to five generations each year. The grayish or brownish caterpillar, 1 to 2 inches (2.5–5 cm) long, rests during the day just beneath the soil near a plant stem. If you turn one up, you'll likely find it curled into a circle.

A cutworm damages seedlings and transplants by coming out at night to wrap itself around the stem and chew or cut through at soil level. The plant top flops over, making this problem easy to confuse with damping off (described on page 115).

To *avoid* cutworms:

- Cultivate twice before planting in spring to expose cutworms to natural predators.
- One week before setting out seedlings, combine BtK with moist bran and molasses and spread it over the planting area to attract and kill larvae.
- Apply an acidic mulch, such as pine needles.
- Poke a toothpick or twig into the ground next to the stem of each transplant, so cutworms can't wrap around the stem and chew through it.
- Spray seedlings with neem.
- Diligently control weeds in late summer and fall.

Natural enemies: beneficial nematodes *(Ineoplectana carpocapsae),* ground beetles, trichogramma wasp *(Trichogramma pretiosum).*

A cutworm wraps around a stem and chews through it at soil level.

Leafhoppers

Leafhoppers *(Circulifer tenellus)* occur throughout North America, but are particularly prevalent in western states. The slender, greenish or brown, wedge-shaped hopper grows up to ½ inch (12 mm) long. At rest it holds its transparent wings over its body, like a tent, but is ready to leap into flight at the slightest disturbance. The leafhopper overwinters in weeds and produces several generations each year by depositing its yellowish eggs in plant stems. Nymphs look like pale adults without wings.

Although both nymphs and adults suck juices from stems and the undersides of leaves, they seldom cause serious damage. They do, however, inject toxic saliva, and a large infestation causes plants to be stunted and have yellow, curled leaves. Leafhoppers also spread viruses.

To *avoid* leafhoppers:

- Protect seedlings with floating row covers until vines begin to blossom.
- Partially shade vines in hot weather — leafhoppers like full sun.

To *control* leafhoppers:

- Spray both sides of infested leaves with plain water, then with insecticidal soap (add 1 tablespoon of isopropyl alcohol per quart [15 ml/L] to help penetrate the leafhopper's tough shell); repeat in one week.
- Apply neem, pyrethrins, or rotenone only if infestation is serious — mobile leafhoppers are difficult to control with insecticides.
- Remove weed and garden debris at season's end.

Natural enemies: various flies and wasps.

Leafminers

Leafminers are the larvae of tiny black and yellow flies of various *Liriomyza* species in the Agromyzidae family found throughout the United States. The flies lay clusters of white eggs on the undersides of leaves, producing several generations per year. Eggs hatch into stubby, tiny (0.04 inch, 1 mm), yellowish maggots that tunnel through tender leaves, occasionally appearing as bulges inside a leaf.

They create winding trails that cause leaves to eventually dry up. They don't seriously affect a mature vine, but they can destroy a seedling. After feeding, the maggots fall to the soil to pupate. Adults emerge in early summer as small (0.08 inch, 2 mm) flies to begin a new cycle.

To *avoid* leafminers:

- Cultivate the soil in fall and spring to expose pupae to natural predators.

To *control* leafminers:

- Set out sticky traps.
- Find and crush eggs.
- Pinch off and burn larvae-infested leaves.
- Use neem to control larvae in leaves.
- Notice what date vines become infested and anticipate the arrival of leafminers in the future by applying floating row covers.

Natural enemies: birds, parasitic wasps.

Spider Mites

Spider mites *(Tetranychus urticae)* are minute, greenish yellow, eight-legged creatures that suck juices from the undersides of leaves, weakening the plant and slowing its growth. The leaves turn pale green and become covered with yellow pinprick spots. Additional evidence of spider mites is their fine silky webs.

When the weather is warm and dry, the mites lay tiny, translucent eggs and multiply rapidly, producing 10 or more generations each season. Infestations begin in grassy areas, particularly around the edges of a field. Mowing encourages the mites to migrate to cultivated vines. A mite outbreak may also follow the continuous use of chemical insecticides such as Furadan, Sevin, and pyrethroids.

To *control* spider mites:

- Spray tops and bottoms of leaves with water once a week.
- Spray heavily with insecticidal soap, then cover vines with a sheet for three days to hold in moisture and block out light; repeat five days later.

Natural enemies: various predatory mites and beetles, ladybugs, thrips.

Squash Bugs

The dark brown to black squash bug *(Anasa tristis)* appears throughout the United States shortly after vines begin to run. This bug is easy to recognize by its shield shape, the triangular design on its flat back, and the peculiar odor it emits when crushed. Because of the latter trait, it's also called stinkbug.

The ½- to ¾-inch (1–2 cm) adults overwinter in tree bark, weeds, and woodpiles, emerging in spring to feed on young vines and to lay clusters of shiny, reddish brown eggs on the undersides of leaves. The eggs hatch in about 10 days to produce one generation per year.

Both the adults and their nymphs — yellowish green, teardrop-shaped teenagers — pierce leaves to suck juices from them, and inject toxic substances that cause leaves to rapidly wilt, dry out, and turn black. A serious infestation can kill a young vine.

To *avoid* squash bugs:

- Plant nasturtiums and petunias to repel them.
- Plant zucchini nearby to lure squash bugs from pumpkin vines.
- Protect young vines with floating row covers.

To *control* squash bugs:

- Handpick early adults appearing on leaves.
- Crush egg clusters laid on the undersides of leaves.
- Lay boards alongside vines; in the early morning, lift the boards and smash the bugs congregated there.
- Spray vines with tea brewed from cedar chips.

- If adults become numerous, apply sabadilla dust to the upper and undersides of leaves.
- Control nymphs with rotenone.
- Burn vines at the end of the season.

Natural enemies: various parasitic wasps and flies, including the tachinid fly *(Trichopoda pennipes).*

Vine Borers

Squash vine borers *(Melittia cucurbitae)* appear when vines begin to run. They are common east of the Rocky Mountains, but are not often a problem in extreme northern areas. The borer is a fat, 1-inch-long (2.5 cm), brown-headed white caterpillar, the offspring of a ¾-inch (2 cm) moth with dark front wings, clear hind wings, and a red abdomen. The adult looks less like a moth than like a fly or wasp, and makes a buzzing sound while flitting, much like a dragonfly, during the heat of the day.

Vine borers lay single eggs in late spring or early summer, producing one or two generations a year. The poppy-seed-sized eggs — laid along the stem near the base of a vine — are flat, oval, and brown. In about a week larvae emerge and bore holes to enter a stem to feed. You'll know one is in there if you see a small hole in the stem and a pile of greenish plant sawdust, or frass (excrement), beneath the hole. The vine wilts suddenly, rots, and dies. Since damage starts on the inside of the stem, it can be hard to spot before it's too late.

Prepare ahead for vine borer by fertilizing vines to induce vigorous growth, and by burying leaf nodes along the runners to encourage auxiliary roots — if a borer gets in near the main root, supplemental roots may save the plant. Keeping vines buried discourages borers in another way: They generally enter stems within 6 inches (15 cm) of the soil level, but they won't enter beneath the soil.

Slitting a stem to find and destroy a borer is time consuming and ineffective, and opens the way to disease. Instead, remove and destroy badly damaged runners.

To *avoid* vine borers:

- Cultivate the soil several times before planting.
- Plant borer-resistant cultivars.

- Select a short season cultivar and plant it late in the season.
- Protect vines with floating row covers until female flowers appear.
- Discourage egg laying by winding an old nylon stocking or other piece of cloth around the lower 6 inches (15 cm) of the plant's stem.

To *control* vine borers:

- Find and crush eggs.
- Spray the bottom 6 inches (15 cm) of stem bases weekly with BtK or pyrethrins and rotenone, to kill emerging larvae.
- Inject an infested stem with BtK or predatory nematodes, squirted in with an eyedropper or syringe.
- Burn infested vines.

Natural enemies: beneficial nematodes.

Whiteflies

Gnatlike whiteflies *(Trialeurodes vaporariorum)* occur primarily in areas where winters are warm, or on greenhouse-grown plants. Usually you can't tell that a vine is infested unless you disturb the leaves and see a cloud of tiny, white-winged insects fluttering in all directions. A few white-flies cause little damage. In the Southwest, however, the sweet potato whitefly spreads squash mosaic virus.

Wingless, translucent larvae suck juices from the undersides of leaves, weakening plants. They also secrete a sticky honeydew on which a sooty black fungus grows. Both the whiteflies and their honeydew can easily be washed off with plain water.

To *avoid* whiteflies:

- Start seeds indoors only in an area that's free of whiteflies, or seed directly outdoors.
- Protect seedlings with floating row covers until blossom time.

To *control* whiteflies:

- Rinse off leaves of infested seedlings with plain water, then spray with insecticidal soap or neem.
- If all else fails, apply pyrethrins or rotenone.

Natural enemies: predatory beetles, parasitic wasps *(Enscarsia formosa).*

Diseases

Pumpkin diseases tend to appear in the fall when temperatures remain below 50°F (10°C) for days at a time, weakening the plant's cell walls and opening the way for diseases to enter. Diseased pumpkin vines may wilt and die, or they may continue growing to produce fruit with poor flavor and texture.

Diseases that affect pumpkin vines run the gamut from bacteria to viruses to fungi, none of which harm humans. Bacterial and viral infections are spread primarily by traveling insects, so your efforts to control insects will also control diseases. Fungi, which are spread mainly by wind, and which flourish in moist environments, can be minimized by watering vines only in the early morning, so the leaves have time to dry out before evening. Better yet, apply water only to the surrounding soil, never to the leaves or vines.

Since you can spread diseases via your hands, clothing, or tools, take precautions after handling diseased vines: Wash your hands and disinfect your gardening tools with a solution of chlorine bleach, mixed 3 table-spoons per quart of warm water (45 ml/L).

Diagnosing Disease

When you try to diagnose a pumpkin-vine disease you may find individual symptoms to be confusingly similar from disease to disease; instead, look for combinations of symptoms. Examine leaves, stems, and fruits, as well as the vine as a whole. For example, did the whole vine suddenly wilt, or was it just one runner?

If you find symptoms that seem to indicate two or more different diseases, quite likely that's exactly what you have. Once a vine is initially weakened, diseases tend to follow one another. If things get out of hand, sometimes the best course of action is to pull up and burn the vines, and take measures to prevent a recurrence the following year.

Angular Leaf Blight

Angular leaf blight, or angular spot disease, is caused by *Pseudomonas syringae* bacteria, which overwinter in plant debris that

Signs of Disease

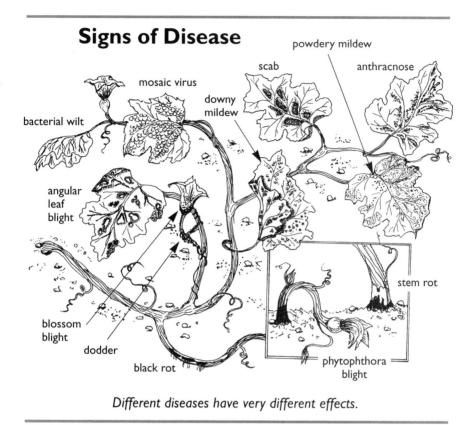

Different diseases have very different effects.

has been tilled into the soil. The bacteria survive in soil for up to two years and are spread by irrigation water. The disease affects cucumbers and watermelons more often than pumpkins, but may infect pumpkins, especially in hot weather when conditions are damp.

The bacteria are most likely to take hold in the early morning when leaves are covered with dew, but they may also appear after a heavy rain or after vines have been dampened by overhead watering. First a series of small, angular spots appears on the leaves, especially along the veins. Later the spots get brown, dry, and crisp, then fall out, leaving lacy holes.

To *avoid* angular leaf blight:

- Avoid overhead watering.
- Avoid high-nitrogen fertilizer, which increases a vine's susceptibility.
- Remove and destroy vines at the end of each season.
- Practice a three-year crop rotation.

To *control* angular leaf blight:

- At the first sign of disease, pull up and burn infected vines, or
- thoroughly wet vines with bordeaux mixture and repeat every 5 to 10 days.
- Do not save seeds from infected vines.

Anthracnose

Anthracnose is caused by *Colletotrichum lagenarium* fungi that live in plant debris, especially in straw bedding turned into the soil with livestock manure. The fungi can survive in the soil for up to five years, more often infecting cucumber, melon, or watermelon plants than pumpkin vines. Fungi become active in moderately warm, wet weather, spread by insects and by splashing or dripping water from rain or sprinklers.

Signs of anthracnose are brown patches that extend along leaf veins. The patches may lighten at the centers as they dry and turn crisp, then crumble to leave holes. Stems first ooze a gummy, oily substance, and later develop yellow or tan streaks that turn brown with decay. Fruits may have small, dark, sunken oily spots on which pink, gelatinous spore masses appear in wet weather.

To *avoid* anthracnose:

- Plant resistant cultivars.
- Avoid overhead watering.
- Remove and destroy vines at the end of each season.
- Rotate crops.

To *control* anthracnose:

- Remove and destroy seriously infected vines, or
- apply bordeaux every 10 days and after every rain.
- Do not save seeds from infected vines.

Bacterial Wilt

Bacterial wilt (BW) is caused by *Erwinia tracheiphila* bacteria, which more commonly infect cucumbers and melons than pumpkins. While most pumpkin varieties are fairly tolerant, the disease sometimes surfaces in the central United States, spread by cucumber beetles that travel from plant to plant as they feed. The disease is not transmitted through seeds.

First several leaves wilt, then entire runners. Often the whole plant seems to wilt and die overnight, the fast-acting bacteria having plugged the stem's water vessels, choking the vine. You'll know it's bacterial wilt if you cut a stem and find a clear, sticky, mucous oozing substance that forms a thread as you gently pull the cut ends apart.

To *avoid* bacterial wilt:

- Control cucumber beetles, especially when vines are in the seedling stage.

To *control* bacterial wilt:

- Pull up and destroy infected plants — they cannot recover.

Black Rot

Black rot (BR), also called fruit rot and gummy stem blight, is caused by *Didymella bryoniae* fungi that live on dry plant debris on or in the soil, where they can survive for more than a year. The fungi thrive in warm, humid weather and thus are more common in southern climates. They are most likely to infect damaged or stressed vines, especially if leaves remain wet or if water puddles near the stem. Tests at Wye Research and Education Center in Queenstown, Maryland, indicate that controlling cucumber beetle also minimizes black rot.

These fungi cause stems to develop soft, moist patches that first ooze a reddish brown, gummy fluid (hence the term "gummy stem blight"), later becoming covered with gray-blue mold, then drying to a tan color. Pale brown

Avoid black rot by controlling cucumber beetles.

patches develop on the edges of leaves, working toward the center until the entire leaf wilts and dies. If the plant's crown rots, the entire vine will die. The fruit rot stage occurs at the time fruits start to form, when young pumpkins develop circular green patches of rot that later turn dark brown. Typical of this disease are black dots on all rotting areas.

To *avoid* black rot:

- Avoid overhead watering and standing puddles.
- Control cucumber beetles.
- Remove and burn vines at the end of each season.
- Deeply cultivate the soil and plant a cover crop.
- Solarize the soil.
- Practice at least a two-year crop rotation.

To *control* black rot:

- Use an old toothbrush to scrub off soft stem spots in the early stages; rinse with plain water and dry well.
- Spray with a general fungicide every 7 to 10 days, starting when fruits begin to form; seasonally rotate fungicides from different chemical families to avoid developing resistant fungi.
- Remove and destroy infected foliage and fruit.
- Do not save seeds from infected vines.

Blossom Blight

Blossom blight, also called chanephora fruit rot, is caused by the soil-borne *Choanephora cucurbitarum* fungus found in hot, humid climates. This fungus lives in the soil on plant debris, where it can survive for many years to surface during warm, wet weather. It's spread by insects and wind, and by splashing rain or irrigation water. It usually invades a vine through some injury, such as an insect puncture or a growth split that occurs when heavy rains follow a drought or when plants are watered irregularly.

Besides colonizing a wound, the fungi may enter through a wilting blossom. The first sign is rapidly decaying blossoms, both male and female. Soon lots of black pinpoint spots appear on the flowers and fruit, starting at the blossom end. Fungicides are rarely effective.

To *avoid* blossom blight:

- Grow vines on mounds with plenty of room between them.
- Improve air circulation by controlling weeds and thinning vines.
- Water regularly and never late in the day.
- Prevent standing puddles.
- If conditions remain wet, remove all blossoms until the weather clears.
- Keep fruits away from direct soil contact.
- Rotate crops.

To *control* blossom blight:

- Cut off and burn affected parts.
- Do not save seeds from infected vines.

Damping Off

Damping off, also called collar canker or root rot, is caused by several species of *Pythium* and *Phytophthora* fungi that can survive in the soil for as long as 12 years and attack newly emerged seedlings of all kinds. This disease is most likely to appear when seeds take a long time to germinate, perhaps because they were planted too deeply or the soil is too cool, too heavy, or highly compacted. The fungi thrive in and are spread by water, especially where drainage is poor and/or plants are crowded.

Damping-off causes stems to collapse in newly emerged seedlings, yellowing and dried leaves in slightly older plants.

The classic sign of damping off is a rotten stem that looks dark and pinched at the soil level, causing the plant to collapse and die. A slightly older plant may not collapse; instead, its leaves become yellow and dry, and its roots appear yellowish or brownish and rotting.

To *avoid* damping off, plant seeds treated with a fungicide such as sulfur or Captan, or one of these homemade preparations:

Crush a couple of garlic cloves, stir them into a pint (0.5 L) of water, strain out the garlic, and soak seeds in the water for a few hours before planting them.

Add 5 teaspoons chlorine bleach per pint (25 ml/0.5 L) of water, soak the seeds for 90 seconds, rinse them in clear water, and plant.

Additional avoidance measures:

- Germinate seeds in a sterile planting medium.
- Keep seedlings from crowding one another.
- Water seedlings with garlic water (one peeled, crushed garlic clove per quart/liter, set aside overnight and then strained).
- Avoid overwatering.
- Transplant seedlings only into warm soil.

To *control* damping off:

- Start applying fungicide early in the season; prevent development of resistant strains of fungi by seasonally rotating fungicides from different chemical families.
- Remove and destroy dead plants.

Downy Mildew

Downy mildew (DM) is caused by *Plasmopara* fungi that thrive in damp weather when temperatures range between 45 and 55°F (7–13°C) for more than a month. Because the fungi prefer low temperatures, this disease is more serious in the North than in the South. It usually appears around mid-August, but sometimes as early as mid-July, spread by insects, wind, and splashing rain or irrigation water.

The fungi cause patches to appear between the veins of usually older leaves. The patches start out yellow, then become tan or brown with white or gray downy fuzz underneath. As the disease worsens, the patches turn soot black. Infected plants grow poorly or may shrivel and die. Fruit, if it develops at all, is likely to be tasteless.

To *avoid* downy mildew:

- Plant tolerant cultivars.
- Grow vines on mounds with plenty of space between them.
- When conditions are right for this disease to occur, heavily spray vines with compost tea.
- Practice a three-year crop rotation.

To *control* downy mildew:

- Remove and burn infected leaves.
- Spray with bordeaux every five to seven days from the time vines start to run, or
- starting at the first sign of downy mildew, spray with compost tea every two weeks.

Mosaic Virus

Three viruses seriously affect pumpkins: cucumber mosaic, squash mosaic, and watermelon mosaic. Symptoms are similar for all three: Leaves become puckered and misshapen. Leaf edges curl and get crisp. The areas surrounding leaf veins turn light green, then yellow as the leaf deteriorates. New leaves are stunted and crumpled. Vine growth is stunted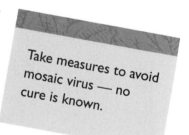
(vine stems are short between leaf stems). Fruits may not develop; any that grow are bumpy, deformed, and light in color.

Take measures to avoid mosaic virus — no cure is known.

None of these symptoms appears until a week or two after the vine is infected, so by the time you notice that anything is wrong, the disease has already spread. No cure is known for mosaic virus. Remove and burn infected plants.

Cucumber mosaic virus (CMV) is the virus that most commonly infects pumpkin vines. It is widely distributed throughout North America, but most often occurs in warm climates. Besides cucurbits, it attacks tomatoes, peppers, lettuce, spinach, and a variety of weeds. Carried by aphids, it appears just after vines begin to run.

Squash mosaic virus (SqMV) is also found throughout North America, most commonly where cucumber beetles are rampant. It is transmitted by means of contaminated seeds, and thus may appear in seedlings. The virus spreads when cucumber beetles and other chewing insects become contaminated while feeding on infected weeds or pumpkin vines, then move on to feed on healthy vines. It is also spread by infected leaves that rub against healthy leaves, and by the tools and hands of a gardener who has been working around infected vines.

Watermelon mosaic virus (WMV) occurs in warm weather when the humidity is high, and is spread by aphids and spider mites. In addition to cucurbits, it attacks peas, beans, spinach, and a variety of weeds.

Zucchini yellow mosaic virus (ZYMV) is a fourth type of mosaic. It's not as serious for pumpkins as the other three, but it may cause green spots to appear on the shells of miniature pumpkins grown near summer squash.

To *avoid* mosaic virus:

- Plant resistant cultivars.
- Control insects.
- Control weeds in and surrounding your pumpkin patch.
- Avoid including other susceptible crops in your rotation plan.

To *control* the spread of mosaic virus:

- Remove and burn infected vines.
- Disinfect tools after working around infected vines.
- Do not save seeds from infected vines.

Powdery Mildew

Powdery mildew (PM), also called oidium, is caused by several related fungi, most commonly *Erysiphe cichoracearum,* found throughout North America. The disease is likely to appear anytime from mid-July through the end of the season. Warm weather coupled with high humidity, rainfall, or dew activates dormant spores that have been anchored to living plants for the winter. The spores, spread by insects and wind, are less likely to infect vines whose leaves don't remain damp overnight.

When a spore lands on a pumpkin leaf, it germinates and attaches itself within hours. As it grows, it deposits new spores that look like spots of flour on the stems and on both sides of the leaves. Eventually entire leaves become coated with the powdery dust. Sometimes patches of tiny black dots also appear. The spores, in turn, get blown onto new leaves, spreading rapidly by producing a new generation every 5 to 10 days.

The fungus draws moisture from the leaves, causing them to dry out and die. Fruits on the vine may ripen early, be watery, and have a bad taste or no flavor at all. The disease is most serious when days are hot and nights are cool. In extreme cases, it can kill the vine.

To *avoid* powdery mildew:

- Plant resistant cultivars.
- Control insects.
- Avoid overhead watering.
- Water only in the morning.
- Apply water to the soil only, not to the leaves.
- Thin leaves to improve air circulation.
- Anticipate the appearance of this disease by heavily spraying vines with compost tea or a baking soda solution (see below).
- Remove and destroy vines at the end of each season.
- Seasonally rotate resistant pumpkin varieties (powdery mildew can mutate and infect once-resistant varieties).

To *control* powdery mildew:

- Remove and burn infected vine parts; disinfect the pruning shears after each cut.
- At the first sign of disease, heavily spray the tops and bottoms of leaves with compost tea every two weeks, or
- heavily spray every two weeks with a baking soda solution — 4 teaspoons of baking soda and 4 teaspoons of dishwashing liquid to 1 gallon of warm water (20 ml each of baking soda and dishwashing liquid/4 L of water) — or
- apply sulfur weekly; to avoid burning leaves, check the label for instructions pertaining to pumpkin vines, and apply sulfur only when the temperature is below 80°F (27°C).

Phytophthora Blight

Phytophthora blight — also called root rot, crown rot, or fruit rot — is a serious disease of mature vines. It is caused by the soilborne fungus *Phytophthora capsici,* one of the many fungi that cause damping off in seedlings. Phytophthora blight occurs when temperatures are above 65°F (18°C) and soil moisture is high, commonly after 2 inches (5 cm) or more of rainfall.

A rotting crown can cause the entire vine to wilt and die at any time during the growing season following a period of soil saturation. Most likely to succumb are vines that are stressed — because they have too many fruits, for example, or have suffered root loss through improper cultivation. A pumpkin lying in a puddle may rot, starting on the side touching the ground. Additional signs include: brown dead patches, sometimes ringed with yellow, on young leaves; and brown, sticky, rotting blossoms attached to young fruit.

The disease spreads rapidly after heavy rains. Once it shows up in your pumpkin patch, expect to see it year after year. Fungicides have little effect, because of the difficulty of spraying all parts of a mature vine.

To *avoid* phytophthora blight:

- Ensure good drainage to prevent standing water around the bases of plants.
- Grow compact vines on mounds; grow spreading vines on flat ground.
- Harvest pumpkins as soon as they mature.
- Do not include other cucurbits, eggplants, or peppers in your crop rotation.

To *control* phytophthora blight:

- Begin spraying with fungicide in midseason and continue spraying every two weeks; seasonally rotate products from different chemical families to prevent the development of resistant strains of fungi.

Phytophthora blight occurs when air temperature and soil moisture are both high.

Scab

Scab, also called gummosis or gray anthracnose, is caused by the soilborne fungus *Cladosporium cucumerinum* found in cool, wet climates. It survives on old vines and fruit left on the vine or turned into the soil; thus, it's most likely to appear where pumpkins are grown on the same ground year after year. The fungi favor wet conditions and temperatures in the 60 to 70°F (15–20°C) range, usually occurring in late summer when nights turn cool and dew is heavy. The disease develops rapidly and is spread by wind, by insects, and by the hands and tools of gardeners who handle infected vines.

Leaves may develop somewhat angular grayish spots encircled in brown and sometimes surrounded with a yellow halo. In damp weather the spots may be covered with green mold. Elongated brown spots appear on stems, sometimes oozing an oily substance. Shells develop sunken moist spots that scab over in warm weather to become dry and corky, perhaps dark at the center. In cool weather, the scabs ooze and the fruits rot. The scabs may not be noticeable until the pumpkins are brought in and stored under too-cool conditions.

To *avoid* scab:

- Ensure good soil drainage.
- Avoid overhead watering.
- Water only in the morning.
- Begin spraying with fungicide when true leaves form, and repeat every five to seven days.
- Remove and destroy vines at the end of each season.
- Disinfect saved seeds for two minutes in a 2 percent solution of sodium hypochlorite — 1 teaspoon of chlorine bleach per cup of warm water (5 ml/0.25 L).

To *control* scab:

- Remove and burn infected plants, and disinfect garden tools after working around them.
- Do not include other cucurbits in crop rotation, but do include corn to help break the disease cycle.

Stem Rot

Stem rot — also called soft rot or watery rot — is caused by the soil-borne, mushroomlike fungus *Sclerotinia sclerotiorum* found throughout North America. This fungus attacks a wide variety of vegetables including eggplants, lettuce, peppers, tomatoes, and all cucurbits, making crop rotation somewhat ineffective against it.

The fungus survives on crop debris left on the ground, and may remain dormant for years just below the soil's surface. It prefers humus-rich soil and is most likely to flourish in moist, cool climates, often becoming active during fall rains when temperatures start to drop.

The disease first appears as a moist decay spot on a stem, sometimes where the main vine comes out of the ground, or as a round to oblong rotten spot on fruit. The decayed portion becomes covered with a white mass that looks like down or cotton and in places turns brown and gummy, then black.

To *avoid* stem rot:

- Ensure good drainage.
- Plant on mounds, for good air circulation.
- Space vines well apart.
- Avoid overhead watering.
- Separate runners and fruit from soil with black plastic mulch.
- Solarize the soil.
- Do not include eggplants, lettuce, peppers, tomatoes, or non-pumpkin cucurbits in crop rotation.

To *control* stem rot:

- Remove and burn infected vines.
- If the disease spreads, apply a fungicide.

Avoid stem rot by providing good drainage and air circulation.

Other Pumpkin Pests

Rodents and gophers burrow through the soil to come up under a pumpkin and hollow out the insides. I once offered a friend a fine fat specimen growing in my garden. When he went out to harvest his prize, it weighed nothing — the insides had been eaten out by some rodent. To keep rodents from chewing through the bottoms of your ripening pumpkins, place a board beneath each one.

Woodchucks, or groundhogs, relish tender vine ends. They have voracious appetites and can soon put you out of the pumpkin-growing business. The best defenses against a groundhog are an electrified net fence, a frisky garden-guarding dog, or a .22 rifle.

Raccoons will chew through tender immature pumpkins to get at their seeds, and will mar the rinds of larger pumpkins while climbing on top to perch. A radio left on overnight may keep raccoons away, and corn growing nearby will lure them to tastier fruits. If all else fails, trap the critters in a live trap and take them *far* away (preferably to the other side of a river or other large body of water) before releasing them.

Slugs and snails damage soft, tender shells and are most active in damp weather, when they can be handpicked in the early morning or early evening. To deter slugs and snails:

- Set each pumpkin on a bed of builder's sand (which serves the additional purpose of keeping the fruit off damp soil).
- Liberally spread diatomaceous earth or wood ashes around vines; repeat every time you water or it rains.
- Trap slugs and snails with beer, or bread yeast mixed with water, placed in a pan with straight sides, nestled into the soil with its rim at ground level. The slimy creatures will come for a drink, fall in, and drown.
- Lay boards around your vines and turn them over each morning to destroy the slugs and snails hiding underneath. To kill the slugs and snails, every night before you lay the boards down coat the undersides with petroleum jelly liberally sprinkled with salt.
- Lure slugs and snails into a partially overturned clay flowerpot baited with bran; gather them from inside the pot in the morning.

Dodder is a parasitic weed of many species in the Cuscutaceae family. It sprouts from a seed and looks like a thick, bright yellow or orange thread as it winds around the nearest plant, which may well be a pumpkin vine. Eventually dodder detaches itself from the soil and attaches suckers to young stems, from which it drains nutrients.

Pumpkin Problems at a Glance

Plant part	Symptom	Problem*
Leaves	Ashen green with yellow pinpricks; silky webs on leaf undersides	Spider mites
	Chewed through with winding trails	Leafminers
	Yellowish brown patches on top, fuzzy patches underneath	Downy mildew
	Turn yellow; undersides coated with sticky black soot	Whiteflies
	Turn yellow, curl, and pucker	Aphids
	Angular spots, turn brown with lacy holes	Angular leaf blight
	Wilt rapidly, turn crisp and black	Squash bugs
	Wilt	Vine borers
	Turn brown and curl at edges	Leafhoppers
	Brown patches or holes along veins	Anthracnose
	Yellow and chewed with holes	Cucumber beetles
	Rolled	Borers (pickleworms)
	Sprinkled with fine white powder	Powdery mildew
	Pucker, curl, turn crisp	Mosaic virus
	Die from the edges inward	Black rot
	Gray spots encircled with brown	Scab
New leaves	Grow stunted and crumpled	Mosaic virus
Young leaves	Yellow-ringed brown patches	Phytophthora blight
Young plants	Die suddenly	Squash bugs
Seedling stem	Collapses at soil level	Damping off; cutworms
Stem	Chewed through or rotted at ground level; piles of green "sawdust" on the ground	Vine borers
	Oozing brown streaks	Scab or Anthracnose
	Full of sticky mucus	Bacterial wilt
	Areas of moist decay	Stem rot

Until it attaches to the vine, dodder is relatively easy to remove and destroy. After it penetrates the vine, though, the only way to get rid of it is to pull up and burn the whole pumpkin plant. If you let dodder grow, it will develop clusters of tiny white flowers that produce an abundance of seeds to sprout another year.

Plant part	Symptom	Problem*
Stem *(cont.)*	Oozes gummy, reddish brown fluid	Black rot
Vine	Grows stunted	Leafhoppers
	Dies suddenly	Vine borers
	Rots at crown, wilts, and dies	Phytophthora blight
	Loses vigor	Powdery mildew
	Grows stunted	Mosaic virus
	Rots at crown and dies	Black rot
Nearly mature vine	Wilts and dies suddenly	Bacterial wilt
Blossoms	Form, but no fruit set (male blossoms don't set fruit)	Poor pollination
	Decay rapidly	Blossom blight
	Chewed	Borers (pickleworms)
	Rot where attached to young fruit	Phytophthora blight
Fruit shells	Blemished	Cucumber beetles
Fruits	Dark oily or pink gelatinous spots	Anthracnose
	Misshapen, other symptoms present	Disease
	Misshapen, no other symptoms	Poor pollination
	Black pinpoint spots at stem end	Blossom blight
	Tunneled through	Borers (pickleworms)
	Round spots coated with "cotton"	Stem rot
	Watery and lack flavor	Powdery mildew
	Bumpy and mottled	Mosaic virus
	Sunken, circular spots	Scab
	Develop green or dark brown circles	Black rot

*To diagnose a problem, look for a combination of symptoms, rather than one symptom alone.

– 6 –
Pumpkin Arts and Crafts

Carving jack-o'-lanterns survives and flourishes as an American folk tradition because it's fun and easy for both adults and children.

— Sam Gendusa
Arts & Activities, 1989

THE JACK-O'-LANTERN HAS ITS ORIGINS in an Irish folk tale. It seems a fellow named Jack was barred from heaven because he was a stingy drunkard, and he was barred from hell because he was so mischievous that he had once played a trick on the devil himself. Jack was, instead, condemned to walk the earth until Judgment Day carrying a lantern to light his way.

Jack's lantern, lit with an ember from Satan's supply, was originally made not from a pumpkin, but from a turnip. Pumpkins and turnips both being storable staples, and pumpkins being much easier to carve, it doesn't take much imagination to see how easily the turnip carving of old Ireland evolved into the pumpkin-carving tradition of the New World.

Today, pumpkin arts and crafts go far beyond carving simple jack-o'-lanterns to include pumpkin sculpture, pumpkin centerpieces, pumpkin flower vases, and even pumpkin soap, to scrub your hands clean after a day of work in the pumpkin patch.

126

Jack-o'-Lanterns

For carving, select a pumpkin that's big enough for the design you have in mind. The bigger the pumpkin, the more creativity you can use in developing details. But remember that a really big pumpkin can take hours, or even days, to carve. While a smaller pumpkin doesn't offer as much room for design, it has the advantage of letting you finish more quickly.

Either start with a pattern and look for a pumpkin with a shape that's compatible, or start with the pumpkin's natural shape and find or create a pattern to suit. A round or oblong pumpkin, as opposed to one with a flattened pancake shape, is easier to carve into a face. An even, symmetrical fruit makes a nice face, but an irregular shape enhances the eerie look of a witch or ghost.

The hardness of the pumpkin's shell is another consideration. A soft shell is easier for young people to carve, but a hard-shelled pumpkin such as a 'Spookie', 'Connecticut Field', or 'Turner' holds up better. Of course, you don't want a *really* hard shell — such as those of the 'Kumi Kumi', 'Southern Miner', or 'Xochitlan Pueblo' — which are best reserved for hot-glue decorating (described later in this chapter).

A good carving pumpkin has a flat bottom, so that your creation will stay put and won't roll. If you find an otherwise perfect pumpkin that doesn't have a flat bottom, you can prop its bottom with wooden wedges nailed to a scrap of lumber. Decorate the stand in the same theme as your carving.

Check your chosen pumpkin carefully to make sure it's not bruised — you don't want your carving to rot prematurely. Carefully brush off dried dirt and other debris. If necessary, wash the pumpkin with water and a few drops of bleach, and dry it well.

Cutting the Lid

Cut a hole in the pumpkin either at the top or at the bottom. Traditionally, a lid is cut at the top, around the pumpkin's stem. But since the stem end tends to be thick and tough, some carvers prefer to cut a hole at the bottom. Having the opening at the bottom also lets you easily set your carving over a candle or lightbulb. Still, while a bottom hole works okay for smaller pumpkins, it can weaken a larger fruit and cause it to deteriorate more quickly.

When carving a lid, rather than trying to cut a circle around the stem, you'll find it easier to carve five straight sides. Make one side obviously longer or shorter than the others, so that you can later reposition the lid accurately. Don't be too skimpy with your lid — you'll need plenty of room to get your hand inside the pumpkin to clean it out. Make the lid at least 4 inches (10 cm) in diameter for a small pumpkin, 8 inches (20 cm) for a big one.

Angle the sides of the lid inward, so the lid won't fall into the pumpkin after the edges have dried out in a few days. Cut away the fibrous pulp clinging to the bottom of the lid. If you open your pumpkin from the bottom, just follow the natural ridge and cut straight inward. Discard the cutout bottom.

Pumpkin carving spans the generations and provides an artistic outlet for all levels of skill.

Pumpkin-Carving Tools

Years ago, safety engineer Paul Bardeen of Racine, Wisconsin, made a carving saw by embedding one end of a coping-saw blade into a short piece of wooden dowel. His children found the short, narrow cutting blade easy to use, especially around corners and curves. Bardeen, who enjoyed demonstrating carving for schoolchildren, also adapted drill bits for making holes in the shell.

When Paul Bardeen died in 1983, in his honor his son John founded the family business Pumpkin Masters, which today produces carving tools based on his father's ideas. These and other brands of tools designed to make carving easy and safe are available through many catalogs that sell pumpkin seeds, and may also be found in department stores around Halloweentime.

Tools

You can use the tools normally found in any kitchen or handyman's shop to carve, or you can use tools designed especially for carving pumpkins (see Pumpkin-Carving Tools box on page 128). Many carvers use a strong pocketknife for cutting the initial opening into the pumpkin. Others use a kitchen knife with a long, thin, strong blade. But even the best knife blade may be hard to force through a thick, tough shell, and may break if you twist it. On the other hand, as Paul Bardeen discovered, the back-and-forth motion of a saw or serrated knife lets you more easily and safely penetrate the shell. If you are carving a giant pumpkin, you'll need a larger saw than any you'll find in a carving kit, because the meat ranges from 3 to 8 inches (7.5–20 cm) thick. You might also try an electric meat-carving knife.

Whatever your tool of choice is, for safety's sake keep your free hand away from the tool's cutting edge. In case the tool slips, always carve away from your body, never toward it. And always supervise children who are using even the safest carving tools.

Creating a Design

You can find terrific patterns in a pumpkin-carving pattern book, adapt patterns from a coloring book, or design your own patterns.

If you create an original design that's especially scary, funny, or unusual, it might earn you a cash prize offered in one of the contests listed in the appendix.

If you're artistic, draw your pattern directly on the pumpkin shell with a pencil, china marker (grease pencil), or felt-tip pen, or scratch it on with a nail or the tip of a knife. Most of us have to work out a design on paper first.

As you create your pattern, color in the areas you plan to cut away, so you won't accidentally cut out parts you intended to keep. You also want to make sure ahead of time that cutaway areas don't interconnect to create large open sections that might sag or collapse. For best results, either keep cutout areas fairly small, or leave wide sections between them.

When you're satisfied with your pattern, tape it to your pumpkin so your design won't get messed up by shifting before it's all transferred. Transfer the design by poking a pushpin or nail along the lines at ¼-inch

(6 mm) intervals. Use the pushpin to mark an X in the center of each area you plan to cut away. If you have trouble seeing the dots, connect them with a pencil or the tip of a paring knife, or run a dark felt-tip pen over the dots to bring them out, then use a paper towel to rub off excess ink between dots.

To carve your design, all you have to do is follow the dots. First, though, you'll need to hollow out your pumpkin.

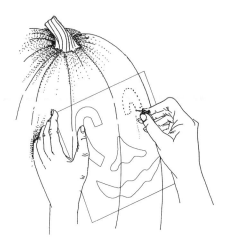

Transfer the design to your pumpkin by taping the pattern to the shell and poking a nail or pushpin along the lines of it to create a dotted image.

Cleaning Out the Pumpkin

Cleaning out a pumpkin is a messy job, best done outdoors or with lots of newspapers to catch the goop. Remove the lid you cut previously, reach in, and pull out as much of the seeds and stringy fibers as you can. Then use an ice cream scoop, strong soup spoon, or pumpkin scooper to scrape the inside wall down to hard flesh.

If you're planning to cut an intricate pattern all the way through the pumpkin, your design will show up better if you scrape away thick areas of flesh until the wall is no more than 1½ inches (4 cm) thick. There's no need to thin the pumpkin's wall if your design will be entirely shaded (cut into the shell, but not through the meat). And you definitely don't want to thin the wall of a giant pumpkin, which would weaken and collapse.

Carving

With your pumpkin hollowed out, you're ready to start carving your design. Use a sharp knife or a carving saw to cut along the dotted lines. Cut straight in, at a 90-degree angle to the shell, so the cutout pieces can easily be popped out with gentle finger pressure. To make a clean corner, cut from one direction to the corner, then start from the other direction and again work toward the corner. Check the job as you go to make sure that all your cuts are straight through to the shell. A jagged cut won't properly let through light, which may spoil your design. A potato peeler works well for cleaning out circles and curves.

Large cutout areas tend to weaken the shell and make it more difficult to work, so begin with smaller features, such as eyes, then move on to larger ones, such as the mouth. If you're carving an intricate pattern, you can avoid breaking through areas that have already been cut away by starting at the center of your design and working toward the outer edges. Within each area, cut from the center outward, and remove larger areas one small section at a time.

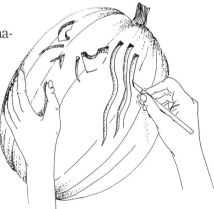

Cut straight in, at a 90-degree angle to the shell.

If your design breaks despite your best efforts, repair the broken piece with sturdy wooden toothpicks. Similarly, you can use wooden toothpicks to attach cutout eyes to the outside of the shell to make ears. Plastic toothpicks, pins, or pieces of wire won't work here because, unlike wooden toothpicks, they don't expand when moist.

Shading and Sculpting

Shading, used alone or in combination with carving, will give your design a three-dimensional look. Shading involves cutting through the shell, but not through the flesh. For example, to create hair, facial wrinkles, and other thin lines, cut a V-channel into the shell using the tip of your knife: First cut along the intended line at an inward angle, then cut a parallel line close to, and angled toward, the first.

For a 3-D look, cut through the shell, but not through flesh.

Creating a design with shading alone lets you carve intricate details that look more like drawing or painting than sculpting. Pumpkin artist Frank Wright and his son Stanley of McEwen, Tennessee, create elaborate designs by scraping away just enough shell to let light glow through carved-out areas. Initially their tools were a low-tech knife and screwdriver; these days they speed things up by using Dremel electric rotary wood-carving tools. The Wrights — who grow and carve 'Aspen', 'Big Max', and 'Connecticut Field' varieties — consider the perfect pumpkin to have a long, wide face. Each man places his pumpkin-in-progress on a rotating turntable, resembling a potter's wheel, with a lock and release to control the table and a foot pedal that raises and lowers the pumpkin as needed.

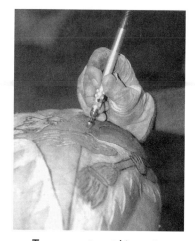

Tennessee pumpkin artist Stanley Wright shades in detail with a Dremel wood-carving tool.

Giant pumpkins appeal to the artistically inclined, whose creations have been called "temporary public art." Sculptor and teacher Sam Gendusa of Dayton, Oregon, considers pumpkin carving to be a fine art, as described in his book *Carving Jack-o'-Lanterns* (listed in the appendix). Gendusa finds that carving the thick flesh of giant pumpkins is quite like carving wood. His tools include a serrated knife to cut the lid and carve out major features, a ¾-inch (19 mm) wood gouge and a mallet or hammer to sculpt finer points, and a potato peeler to scrape away gouge marks

Oregon sculptor Sam Gendusa creates life-like faces using a wood gouge and a mallet.

and to shape details. Gendusa cuts through the flesh only for eyes, nostrils, and mouth, and sculpts such features as eyebrows and laugh lines. The resulting faces are eerily lifelike.

Final Touches

A carved pumpkin usually lasts no more than five days. For best results, carve it the day before you put it on display. To keep your creation from drying out, cover it with a damp towel when it's not on display. If the weather is especially warm and your pumpkin is small enough to fit into the refrigerator, put plastic wrap over the carved design, tilt the lid to let air inside, and store the pumpkin in the refrigerator until you're ready to display it.

If your pumpkin dries out prematurely, you may be able to revive it by soaking it in a tub full of cold water for an hour or two. Don't leave it too long, though, or it may soak up too much water and crack. After soaking, pat the pumpkin dry to minimize rotting.

To make your pumpkin art last longer, wait for half an hour after you finish the carving, then rub the cut areas and inside with a dry cloth and apply a protective coating. You might use petroleum jelly, clear furniture wax, or vegetable oil painted on with a brush. Sam Gendusa sprays each finished piece with several coats of lacquer or hair spray, which gives it a nice glossy finish.

To revive a dried out carved pumpkin, soak it in a tub full of cold water for one to two hours.

Discard your pumpkin as soon as the display is over. If you leave it lying around, it will eventually dissolve into a slimy mess that smells bad, is difficult to clean up, and may damage wood finish or anything else it touches.

Carving Demonstrations

Public demonstrations of pumpkin carving always draw a crowd, whether at a pumpkin festival, harvest fair, crafts show, or farmer's market. Depending on the situation, you might have continuous demonstrations or post a schedule listing the time of each event. Giant-pumpkin carving is interesting, but can take hours and may bore a crowd desiring fast action. Gauge the speed of your demonstrations on whether people will be wandering through and soon leaving (as they would at a farmstand) or wandering back later to check on your progress (as they might at a crafts show). Set up your display so that visitors can take photos of friends and family members with your creations.

Photographing Your Masterpiece

To preserve your masterpiece on film (which is necessary if you wish to enter a national pumpkin-carving contest), place your lighted pumpkin in a room totally dark except for the light glowing from inside the pumpkin. Set your camera on a tripod, choosing an angle from which the pumpkin's light doesn't shine directly into the lens. Take the photo at a slow shutter speed, without a flash. If your camera has an automatic flash, block it with masking tape.

Doug Hales of Noblesville, Indiana, carved, shaded, and photographed this spectacular pumpkin rendition of the tiger mascot of Northwestern High School in Kokomo. For this great shot, Doug used Kodacolor 200 film in his Canon single-lens reflex camera with a 28-mm 1:2.8 wide angle lens, setting the f-stop at 2.8 for 2.5 seconds.

Special Effects

Light. You can light your jack-o'-lantern from the inside with a candle, a flashlight of appropriate size, or an electric lightbulb. Lights are a good choice for public displays where fire codes prohibit the use of live flame. A red light behind the eyes will give your creation a demonic appearance.

Fire. If you choose to light your pumpkin with a candle, take measures to ensure that the candle won't fall over and start a fire. A stubby votive candle is less likely to tip than a taller, thinner candle.

For a small pumpkin with a hole cut into the bottom, place the candle in a sturdy holder and set the pumpkin over it. If the hole is cut into the top, anchor the candle by poking a nail into the bottom of the pumpkin, through the flesh, then push the candle firmly onto the nail. For a large pumpkin with thick flesh, use a safety candleholder that twists like a corkscrew into the meat at bottom of the shell. Safety candleholders are available from the same sources as pumpkin-carving tools (see the appendix).

A safety candle holder lets you light your pumpkin without burning your fingers or tipping the candle over.

A screw-in candleholder has the advantage of letting you tilt the pumpkin for easy lighting without knocking your candle over or scorching your fingers. If you don't use a screw-in holder, light your candle with a long fireplace match or a regular stick match taped to a barbecue skewer and lit with a second match. To avoid burned fingers, light the candle through an eyehole or other cutout, rather than from the top.

The first time you light the candle, let it burn a few moments with the lid on, then lift the lid and bore a hole into the blackened portion to create a chimney. If your pumpkin is bottomless, and therefore has no lid, you still need to drill a hole into the top, at the spot where flesh has been blackened by the candle. Without a chimney, your candle will get too little oxygen to burn properly, causing it to either smoke or go out.

Scent. To make your jack-o'-lantern smell yummy, sprinkle a little cinnamon or nutmeg into the lid (or the inside top of a bottomless lantern). When you light the candle, you'll magically smell the scent of pumpkin pie.

Smoke. To make your creation breathe fire, immerse a chunk of dry ice in a bowl of warm water on the floor of the pumpkin. The resulting vapor looks just like smoke and can be used to enhance the ghoulishness of a skull or ghost face. When combined with indirect lighting, it can create the impression of movement.

A fogging machine, available from a rental agency, lets you control the vapor so it comes mainly through the nostrils. The machine has a built-in container for warm water into which you drop blocks of dry ice,

Lighted Lantern Safety Tips

Keep candlelit lanterns away from billowing curtains and other fabrics, including children's costumes. Display them in a safe place — on the porch floor, for instance, not on the railing where a child or cat might knock them down. Never leave a candlelit lantern unattended.

and a fan that forces the resulting smoke into a hose. Position the hose through a hole in the back of the pumpkin and aim it so your creature looks like it's breathing fire.

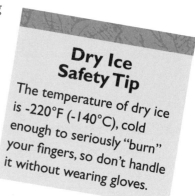

Dry ice is not available in all areas, so check the Yellow Pages for your nearest dealer. This clear, white, nearly odorless crystalline substance evaporates into gaseous carbon dioxide as it melts, leaving no messy puddle as regular ice does (that's why it's called "dry"). It weighs less than regular ice and comes in rectangular chunks wrapped in brown paper to slow evaporation.

Sound. For neighborhood parties or public events, hide a microphone inside your pumpkin and have someone talk to passersby. The person might be concealed at a distance or hiding behind a nearby curtain or partition while peering through a peephole. Talking pumpkins are a big hit at parties where each child is known and can be called by name as he or she comes near the pumpkin "person" — carved from a pumpkin about the size of a human head and set atop a scarecrow stuffed with straw or towels, either seated or stiffened with a broom handle and propped against a wall.

PHOTO BY CECIL E. DORNEY

A child is intrigued when a talking pumpkin knows his name and other personal things about him.

Pumpkin Painting and Decorating

Children under the age of nine lack the coordination to use carving tools safely. They may, instead, be encouraged to paint "spooktacular" faces. A painted pumpkin lasts longer than a carved pumpkin, but, like a carved pumpkin, it's no longer fit for eating (due to the possibility that the pumpkin flesh may absorb paint toxins). Halloween paint sets appear in department stores in September and October. Acrylics, poster paints, or model enamel may also be used.

Kids enjoy painting miniature pumpkins because they're so easy to handle. Especially suitable for painting are the creamy white-shelled mini 'Baby Boo' and the larger 'Lumina'. Here are some tips:

- Plan your design so everything of the same color can be painted at one time.
- Give the first color time to dry, then paint the next color.
- To keep things moving along, work on several pumpkins at once so you can paint one while another dries.
- Add hats and other accessories to enhance painted faces.

The addition of curly ribbon hair and black pointed hats turns mini pumpkins into darling little witches.

Personal Pumpkins

Children love to see their own names painted on or carved into a pumpkin. Sheets of block letters (available from an office supply store or the stationery department of a discount store) designed for spray painting are ideal for carving, because each letter is made up of interconnected areas. Children are delighted to see their names highlighted when light glows through the letters.

Painting needn't be limited to faces. Carol Kerr of Bowie, Maryland, told me about a pumpkin grower whose jack-o'-lantern crop was ruined by rain. In an effort to salvage her source of income for that year, the farmer painted her smaller pie pumpkins to look like the helmets worn by local high school football teams, and sold them as fast as she could paint them.

As a creative alternative to painting, trim a large pumpkin with produce and other items, using your imagination to imitate facial features such as:

- Round smooth tomatoes or small squash or gourds for eyes
- Pepper halves or mini pumpkins for ears
- A carrot, cucumber, or zucchini nose
- Dried cob corn or red peppers for a mouth
- Corn silk, shredded corn leaves, evergreen boughs, straw, or branches of herbs for eyebrows and hair.

The parts may be attached with strong wooden toothpicks or may be stuck into carved-out holes just large enough to hold them in place.

For lasting decorations, hot-glue dried produce, flowers, and herbs to hard-shelled pumpkins. Linda Drowns of Calamus, Iowa, hot-glues flowers and small dried ears of corn to 'Kumi Kumi' pumpkins for Thanksgiving centerpieces that endure into the middle of February.

Such a centerpiece can be turned into a candleholder by boring a hole into the top to receive a stout candle. Miniature pumpkins — trimmed, painted, or plain — make perfect candleholders. They also make

*Pumpkins can be decorated
with naturals such as
vegetables, flowers,
and herbs.*

catchy place cards, with names painted either directly on the shells or on decorative cards glued to the shells. For a matching vase, remove the top, scallop the edges, and hollow out a tall pumpkin, and fill it with flowers or colorful leaves.

Yard Art

Here in middle Tennessee, pumpkin trees are popular in the fall. In many a front yard you will see miniature pumpkins hanging by their stems from small trees or tall shrubs. Some trees are decorated with pumpkins of one color, others have mixed colors — yellow, orange, and white — and still others are festooned with pumpkins painted with designs or faces.

If you don't have a suitable tree or shrub, you might make a pumpkin pyramid. Start with a large pumpkin at the bottom and stack progressively smaller ones on top, ending with a mini.

Or make a totem pole by stacking carved or painted pumpkin heads of similar size one atop the other. The faces might be fanciful or might be made to represent each member of your family, each pet you own, or each animal on your farm. For stability, remove the lids from all but the top pumpkin, so that each nestles nicely into the one below. Better yet, run an old broom or rake handle down the center to hold them all together.

These pumpkin snails with butternut squash heads appeared at Jackson's Pumpkin Farm, Endicott, NY.

The Bob Webber family, who grow pumpkins near Loretto, Ontario, decorate their yard each year with a huge Pumpkinsaurus made by distributing approximately 100 pumpkins along a welded steel frame 12 feet (3.6 m) tall and 20 feet (6 m) long. The first year they included a nest of ornamental gourd eggs. The next year two of the eggs "hatched" into wonderful little Pumpkinsauruses. Each fall the Webber farm becomes known as Pumpkinsaurus Park and attracts 3,000 to 4,000 visitors.

The Bob Webber family of Loretto, Ontario, created this giant Pumpkinsaurus.

Pumpkin Soap

Pumpkin soap is great fun to make and is a unique and useful gift. If you are interested in learning more about making soap, you'll find two excellent books on the subject listed on page 202. To make soap, you need the following equipment:

- 4- to 6-cup mixing container made of heatproof stoneware glass, enamel, stainless steel, or plastic
- 2-cup heatproof (such as Pyrex) measuring container
- Plastic or wooden long-handled spoon
- Spatula made of plastic, wood, rubber, or stainless steel
- Two candy or meat thermometers
- Eye protection (at the very least wear sunglasses)
- Rubber gloves, pot holders or oven mitts
- Flexible soap molds (margarine tubs, paper cups, plastic cookie box liners, etc.) with a total capacity of 3 cups (0.75 L)
- Plastic or stainless steel measuring spoons
- Essential oils to give your soap a pleasant aroma

Soapmaking Procedure

Expert soapmaker Elaine C. White of Starkville, Mississippi, author of *Soap Recipes,* has developed this foolproof 10-step procedure for making pumpkin soap:

Step 1. Put on eye protection and rubber gloves. Measure the cold water into the 2-cup heatproof container. Stirring with a plastic or wooden long-handled spoon, slowly add the lye. Continue stirring until the lye dissolves. The water will heat up, turn cloudy, and emit fumes — avoid breathing them in. Stir until the solution cools down to 120°F (49°C), using one of the thermometers to measure the temperature.

Step 2. Combine the fats, oils, pumpkin puree, and/or pumpkin seeds in the 4- to 6-cup lye-resistant container and heat on the stove to 120°F (49°C), using the other thermometer to measure the temperature. You may continue to stir. Tip: Fat takes less time to heat up than the lye solution takes to cool down.

Step 3. When the fat mixture and the lye solution are both at 120°F (49°C), move the fat container to the sink, where splatters are easy to contain. Stirring, slowly pour the lye solution into the fat.

Step 4. If the recipe calls for milk, stir it in after the fat and lye have been thoroughly mixed.

Step 5. Continue stirring until the soap "traces" (see box). At first the mixture will be thin and watery, then it will turn thick and opaque. Most soap traces within 45 minutes. Stir constantly for the first 15 minutes, then stir once every 15 minutes until the soap traces.

Step 6. After the soap traces, add aromatic spices and/or essential oils. Stir for a few minutes longer to blend well.

Step 7. Pour the soap into the molds, cover the molds with plastic wrap or waxed paper pressed onto the surface, and wait 24 hours for the soap to harden (48 hours for milk soap).

Step 8. Place the molds in the freezer for three hours. Wearing rubber gloves, release the soap from the mold in the same way that you would release ice cubes from a tray.

Step 9. Space the bars out on a sheet of plastic or thick cardboard and set them aside where they won't be disturbed or handled by children. Until the lye completely reacts with the fat, your soap will be soft, harsh, and fatty, so put it where lye and fats won't cause any damage. Turn the bars every two or three days for three weeks. During this aging period, they will harden and the harshness will decrease to make your soap mild.

Step 10. Enjoy your homemade pumpkin soap.

Tracing

"Tracing" describes the correct consistency of soap pouring into molds. To test for tracing:

- Drip a bit of soap onto the surface of the soap in the stirring bowl; it should leave a small mound, or "trace."
- Draw a line in the soap with a spoon or spatula; for a few seconds a "trace" of the line should remain.

Soap Formulas

Here are Elaine's soap formulas for pumpkin lovers. Each formula makes half a dozen bath-sized bars. The "steps" referred to in the formulas correspond with the appropriate step numbers in the soapmaking procedure on pages 142-143. Note that formulas for metric equivalents can be found in the chart on page 209.

Simple Pumpkin Soap

This is an easy-to-make soap with a silky feel and a lovely pumpkin color.

Step 1: ½ cup cold water
         ¼ cup Red Devil lye granules

Step 2: 2 cups lard
         1 cup pumpkin puree

Step 6: 1½ teaspoons essential oil (any scent)

Tracing time: 45 minutes

Pumpkin Seed Bath Pleasure

Milk and pumpkin seed oil combine in this creamy soap to leave your skin feeling smooth and soft when you bathe.

Step 1: ¼ cup cold water
         ¼ cup Red Devil lye granules

Step 2: 1 cup lard or beef tallow
         1 cup white coconut oil
         ½ cup pumpkin seeds, ground

Step 4: 1 cup cold milk

Step 6: 1½ teaspoons essential oil (any scent)

Tracing time: 1 hour 15 minutes

Pumpkin Grower's Hand Soap

This dark brown cleansing bar has the yummy aroma of pumpkin pie, thanks to spices — which also lend a mild abrasiveness to remove tough dirt and grime from the hands of pumpkin gardeners and other hard workers. Pumpkin seeds contribute oil to soften rough skin .

Step 1: ¾ cup cold water
¼ cup Red Devil lye granules

Step 2: 1 cup lard or beef tallow
1 cup coconut oil
¼ cup pumpkin seeds, coarsely chopped

Step 6: 1 tablespoon pumpkin pie spice
¾ teaspoon clove leaf essential oil

Tracing time: 30 minutes

Safe Lye Handling

For soapmaking, use only 100 percent lye, such as the Red Devil brand, not drain cleaners such as Drano. If you can't find lye locally, you can order it from a soapmaking or chemical supplier. Since ordered lye comes in flakes, rather than granules, measure it by weight (2.4 ounces of flakes equal ¼ cup of granules).

Always wear eye protection when you handle lye, and keep children and animals away from the soapmaking area.

Lye (sodium hydroxide), also known as caustic soda, reacts with some metals, so use only heatproof stoneware, glass, enamel, stainless steel, or plastic containers and utensils. Since lye is caustic enough to remove paint, if you accidentally splash lye or freshly made soap onto a painted surface, immediately wash the surface with water and detergent, rinse well, and wipe dry.

Your homemade soap needs time to cure, during which the lye reacts with fats to create cleansing soap and glycerin. After it has cured, it no longer presents the danger of burning skin or eyes, pitting metal, or blistering painted surfaces.

Pumpkins for Profit

Of all the things you can grow, pumpkins are unique in having the ability to sell themselves. For example, I live on a private road with little traffic, yet I have unintentionally sold pumpkins to passersby who saw our pumpkins growing or spotted them piled after the harvest and asked to buy some. One autumn a neighbor on a similarly remote road piled pumpkins in his front yard and sold over 250 of them. The message is clear: People like pumpkins. Nationwide, pumpkins generate more roadside stands than any other produce, and have the greatest number of festivals dedicated to them.

Growing pumpkins for profit lets you avoid the one problem related to most other produce — developing a market. You'll find eager customers at a farmer's market, roadside stand, or pick-your-own pumpkin patch. Learn about local marketing conditions by joining your state's fruit and vegetable growers' association. Check also with your insurance agent to make sure you're adequately covered to deal with the public.

Pumpkins on display near a well-traveled road virtually sell themselves.

To make a significant income by selling directly to the public, you need:

- A visible location
- Good access roads and parking
- Zoning for retail sales
- Labor to help with harvesting and marketing
- A large number of pumpkins in several varieties
- Signs
- Product and liability insurance
- Willingness to deal with all kinds of people

Entertainment Farming

If you sell directly to the public, you have the opportunity to add value to your product through entertainment farming. Growers who build entertainment into their pumpkin sales attract more customers to their farmstands.

Tim and Jan Valla of Gretna, Nebraska, near Omaha, started out with a diversified pick-your-own operation that refocused over time to become "Valla's Pumpkin Patch," including a Spook Shed, Haunted Farmhouse, Storybook Barn, old-time schoolhouse, small-stock petting corral, picnic area, and Pumpkin Cafe serving "goblin' good food." On a busy afternoon, the Vallas see as many as 4,000 visitors at their farm.

Tim Valla attributes the popularity of his patch to its country setting. "You can buy pumpkins at the store," he says, "but the farm atmosphere attracts people." For urban and suburban families alike, the main attraction is being on a working farm and choosing a pumpkin out of the field in which it grew. The Vallas grow more than two dozen varieties, their most popular being the carving pumpkin 'Howden'.

Mike and Lorie Jensen of Junction City, Oregon, attract buyers to their Lone Pine Farm by offering the "Pumpkin Patch Express" — a horse-drawn hay wagon that brings customers into the fields, and brings pumpkins from the fields to the farmstand. Lin and Allan Ayers also give horse-drawn-wagon rides at their historic Faulkner Farm west of Santa Paula, California, each season attracting more than 20,000 visitors, who come to learn how pumpkins grow and how farm animals are raised.

Many pumpkin patches that focus on farm education for school groups send each child home with a souvenir in the form of a small pumpkin. Some also incorporate pumpkin games, which add fun to the visit and help children retain what they learn. Games might include:

- Finding the biggest or heaviest pumpkin growing in the patch
- Most accurately guessing the weight of a big pumpkin
- Guessing how many miniature pumpkins are in a pile
- Rolling a pumpkin downhill the fastest
- Pinning the nose on the pumpkin (blindfold and spin each child, then see who comes closest to tacking a felt nose to the middle of a painted pumpkin face)
- Stringing the most wet pumpkin seeds with a needle and thread within a given time, say five minutes

Fund-Raising

Many pumpkin festivals are held as not-for-profit fund-raisers. Each October, for instance, the sloop *Clearwater* visits communities along the Hudson River, distributing 60 tons of pumpkins in celebration of the harvest season. Proceeds from the sale of the pumpkins help fund the sloop's function as a floating environmental classroom, educating people about the Hudson River and related waterways.

Vanderbilt Children's Hospital benefits from the proceeds of pumpkin sales at the annual Pumpkin Show on the Wright farm in McEwen, Tennessee. Volunteers help set up the show for weeks ahead, and during the event the rescue squad directs traffic and parking. Visitors may special-order pumpkins in advance, or may select a carved or painted pumpkin from among hundreds lining the driveway and filling a big tent set up for the purpose. Pumpkins depicting cartoon characters and politicians are as eagerly sought as traditional Halloween faces.

Proceeds from Delaware's annual World Championship Punkin' Chunkin' are distributed among several local charities. The event was first held in 1986 when a group of friends wondered how far they could toss a pumpkin. Sponsored by the Roadhouse Steak Joint, the competition is held at the Eagle Crest Aerodrome north of Lewes.

While the two-day event now includes target shooting as well as distance throwing, the keenest rivalry remains in the distance competition, which is separated into three divisions — youth (up to 10 years, and

11–17 years old), human powered, and unlimited. All events involve homemade mechanical devices of one sort or another.

In the human-powered division, pumpkins are tossed by machines that operate on springs, rubber cords, counterweights, or any other device capable of storing power supplied by one human during a maximum period of two minutes. The unlimited division allows machines in three classes: catapult, centrifuge, and air powered. Each contestant gets three throws; only the best out of the three counts. The contest rules are:

1. Pumpkins must weigh between 8 and 10 pounds (3.6–4.5 kg).
2. Pumpkins must leave the machine intact.
3. No part of the machine may cross the starting line.
4. No explosives may be used.

Competition has come a long way since the first winner used a catapult to chunk a pumpkin 50 feet (150 m). A new world record of 2,710 feet (813 m) was set in 1996 by an Illinois air cannon called Aludium Q36 Pumpkin Modulator.

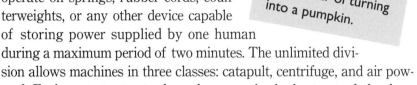

Punkin' Chunkin' World Records

Division	Year Set	By	Distance
Youth, up to 10	1993	unknown	128' 2"
Youth, 11–17	1996	Del Castle Technical High School	759'
Human powered	1996	Gene's Machine	576'
Unlimited	1986	Trey Melson	50'
	1989	John Ellsworth	612'
	1990	Ultimate Warrior	774'
	1991	Ultimate Warrior	776'
	1992	De-Terminator	852'
	1993	Under Pressure	1,204'
	1994	Universal Soldier	2,508'
	1995	Mello Yello New Matik Pumpkin Planter	2,655'
	1996	Aludium Q36 Pumpkin Modulator	2,710'

– 7 –

Pumpkin Eater

Since the pumpkin can be eaten as either a fruit or a vegetable, raw or prepared, and since it can act as its own serving dish and even offers its seeds for a snack or garnish, you can see that it has great versatility as a food.

— Mary Joan Barrett
In Praise of Pumpkins, 1990

PUMPKINS ARE TECHNICALLY CLASSIFIED AS A FRUIT, and most cooks treat them like fruits. But once you start thinking of pumpkin as a vegetable as well as a fruit, you'll more quickly recognize its culinary versatility.

Pumpkin meat is tasty baked, boiled, steamed, or stir-fried. It makes delicious preserves and spicy pickles. It may be dried and eaten as a snack, or ground into flour for baking. Pumpkin blossoms make an attractive garnish, may be added raw to salads, or may be stuffed and batter-fried. Dried pumpkin seeds are a nutritious and healthful snack. Even the tender stems and leaves make savory and nourishing greens.

For cooking, I look for a pumpkin with sweet, firm flesh — sometimes described as fine grained — most often found in Sugar varieties.

Other varieties may cook up thin and bland, or readily turn to mush, which is probably why most recipes call for pumpkin puree. The flesh of a good Sugar pumpkin remains firm when gently steamed or blanched.

Pumpkin Puree

Whenever I puree a pumpkin for a recipe, I always prepare extra to serve as a side dish at supper, topped with butter and perhaps a sprinkling of brown sugar or a few drops of maple syrup. To make a smooth puree from a cooked Sugar pumpkin, mash it with a potato masher, whip it with a whisk, or whirl it in a food processor. Most varieties other than Sugar pumpkins turn to mush with a minimum of stirring in the cooking pot.

Once the meat is mashed, continue to cook it, uncovered, until all the liquid has boiled off. Pumpkin tastes best when it has *just* started to darken, or scorch, but watch carefully that it doesn't burn.

Cooked pumpkin keeps for three to six days in the refrigerator, depending on how cold your unit is and how often you open the door. If you have more puree than you can use right away, pack it into plastic containers, leaving a little headspace for expansion, and freeze it for up to a year.

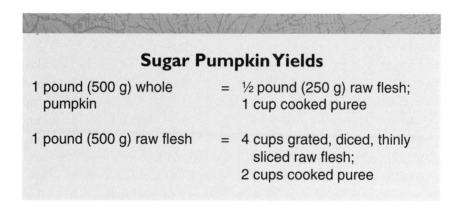

Sugar Pumpkin Yields

1 pound (500 g) whole pumpkin	=	½ pound (250 g) raw flesh; 1 cup cooked puree
1 pound (500 g) raw flesh	=	4 cups grated, diced, thinly sliced raw flesh; 2 cups cooked puree

Peeling a Pumpkin

Different cooks use different methods for extracting meat from a pumpkin. One method is to cut a slice from the bottom, so the fruit will stand firmly upright, then rotate the pumpkin while you peel away the skin from top to bottom. Slice the pumpkin in half and clean out the fibers and seeds. Remove the peel with a good potato peeler or a sharp paring knife.

The method I prefer is to cut the pumpkin into quarters, scrape out the seeds, cut each quarter into wedges, then peel each wedge.

People who hate to peel a pumpkin cook it in the skin: Scrub the shell clean, halve or quarter the pumpkin, scrape out the seeds, steam or bake the pieces, then use a spoon to scrape the soft flesh from the firmer shell.

Cooking Pumpkin

The method you use to cook pumpkin will depend on how much pumpkin you wish to prepare at once, how you wish to use it, how big a hurry you're in, and how important it is not to heat up your kitchen.

Bake peeled 2-inch (5 cm) chunks by brushing them with melted butter, spreading them on a baking sheet, and roasting them at 350°F (175°C) for 45 minutes, or until the flesh is tender enough to be easily pierced with a fork.

To bake unpeeled halves or quarters, place them in a baking pan, cut side down, with about 1 inch (2.5 cm) of water. Bake at 350°F (175°C) until tender, which takes one to two hours, depending on the thickness of the flesh. Serve the flesh in the shell or scrape it from the shell and mash it.

Baking a whole pumpkin will give you drier meat, which saves you time simmering off liquid if your ultimate goal is to make a pie. Stab the pumpkin in at least six places to release steam. Place it on a shallow baking pan covered with water and bake at 350°F (175°C) until the pumpkin is soft enough to give when you push against the shell. How long this takes depends on the size of the pumpkin and the thickness of its flesh; mini pumpkins take about 30 minutes. Cool the fruit, cut it open, scoop out the seeds, and peel away the shell.

Boil peeled chunks or unpeeled sections in salted water for 15 to 20 minutes, or until the meat is tender. Although boiling is one of the fastest ways to cook a pumpkin, it causes some loss of flavor and nutrients.

Steam peeled chunks or unpeeled sections in a steamer over water or in a saucepan containing no more than 1 inch (2.5 cm) of water. Cover and cook for about 30 minutes, or until the meat can easily be pierced through with a fork.

The Healing Pumpkin

Those who claim that pumpkins are not an important food because they contribute few nutrients other than vitamin A miss the point: Pumpkin is one of those rare foods that both tastes delicious and can be eaten by most people in unlimited quantities, since it contains only 50 calories per 1-cup serving with no cholesterol or fat, but has as much fiber as most breakfast cereals.

It's true that pumpkins are a great source of beta carotene, which the human body converts into vitamin A. When pumpkin is eaten daily, its beta carotene and other nutrients help fight infection and heart disease, help ward off some kinds of cancer, and may (according to researchers) slow the effects of aging. Pumpkin seeds, eaten daily, have long been known to help keep the prostate healthy.

Pumpkin historian Mary Joan Barrett discovered that Native Americans used pumpkin to cure kidney infections and rid the body of worms. Other folk cures mentioned in pumpkin literature include the use of pumpkin to combat hemorrhoids, ulcers, dropsy, inflamed intestines, and high blood pressure, and the use of seeds as a cure for bladder infection. Pumpkin tea has been used as a diuretic and a regulator of blood sugar. The Mayans used pumpkin sap to treat burns. Even the leaves may be used — crushed and rubbed on livestock, they repel flies.

Microwave an unpeeled quartered pumpkin, the cut sides covered with plastic wrap. Place the pieces, cut side up, on a paper towel and microwave on high, rearranging the pieces every four minutes. The total cooking time should be about five minutes per pound (0.5 kg), with an additional five minutes standing time.

To microwave a small whole pumpkin, pierce the shell with a fork in several places to let out steam. Cook on high, turning every 4 minutes, for about 20 minutes, or until the flesh is tender. Let stand five minutes before cutting the pumpkin open to remove the seeds and extract the flesh.

To microwave mini pumpkins, hollow them out and wrap each in plastic stretch wrap. Microwave on high for four and a half minutes per pumpkin, rearranging the fruits in the oven every four and a half minutes.

Roast a pumpkin the Native American way — buried in hot campfire ashes.

Culinary Treats

From the time a pumpkin vine starts growing vigorously, it's ready to produce tasty treats. Snip off new shoots at the tips of vines, wash them, and shred them into a saucepan. Cover with water and boil until tender. Drain off the cooking liquid and serve the greens southern-style, sprinkled with crisp bacon bits, or South African–style, sprinkled with finely chopped roasted peanuts. Or stir in a pat of butter or margarine and season to taste with salt and pepper. If you wish, make a smooth puree by whirling the greens in a food processor.

Immature fruits, 2 to 4 inches (5–10 cm) in diameter, may be grated raw into salads, or steamed or stir-fried as you would prepare summer squash. One of my favorite vegetables is baby pumpkin sautéed in butter with a little chopped onion, sprinkled with curry powder.

You might steam shoots with an immature pumpkin and a small onion, both sliced thin. Or thinly slice the pumpkin and an onion, stir-fry until tender but still crisp, and serve on a bed of cooked greens.

In a Pumpkin Shell

A whole pumpkin makes an artful serving dish, especially for a harvest or Halloween party. Wash and dry the shell, cut a wide lid from the top, and scoop out the seeds and stringy fibers. Fill small, uncooked pumpkins with fruit or vegetable salad, cold soup, chip dip, or ice cream. Use a medium- to large-pumpkin as a punch bowl.

A cooked shell makes an attractive bowl for serving hot soups, stews, casseroles, or other prepared foods. To use a hollowed shell for warm food, brush the flesh with a little vegetable oil and sprinkle it with salt and pepper. Place the shell on a baking sheet, with the lid beside it, and bake it at 375°F (190°C) until the flesh is tender, which takes about 20 minutes for a 6-pound (3 kg) pumpkin. Check once or twice for accumulated juice inside the pumpkin, removing it with a turkey baster or large spoon.

When the flesh is just fork-tender, fill the shell with prepared cooked food. Replace the lid and bake the pumpkin 20 minutes more, or until the meat is fully soft. Bring the whole shell to the table and scoop out a little cooked pumpkin with each serving. If you leave the lid on, food will stay warm in the shell for about 20 minutes.

Cooked miniature pumpkins make cute containers for individual servings. Fill them with cranberry sauce, rice or bread stuffing, or pie filling. If you wish, bake the stuffing or pie filling right in the shell.

A sturdy pumpkin shell makes the ideal serving container.

Harvest Brunch

This breakfast-in-a-shell is a favorite of Barbara Schmierer at Stonycreek Farms in Noblesville, Indiana. Unlike farmstand owners who use canned pumpkin or commercially prepared mixes for the treats they offer to the public, Barbara spends a lot of time experimenting with pumpkin recipes so she can explain to her customers the advantages of cooking with fresh pumpkin.

1 3-pound pumpkin	⅓ cup chopped onion
½ teaspoon salt	1 cup sliced mushrooms
¼ teaspoon pepper	1 egg, beaten
1 pound pork sausage	½ cup sour cream
1 tablespoon oil	⅓ cup grated Parmesan
1 cup chopped celery	cheese

1. Preheat oven to 350°F (175°C).

2. Cut the pumpkin in half and remove its seeds. Sprinkle the cavity with the salt and pepper.

3. Place the halves, cut side down, in a large baking pan. Add water to a depth of 1" (2.5 cm). Bake until tender, about 1 hour. Remove from oven and turn halves cut side up.

4. Increase the oven temperature to 375°F (190°C).

5. While the pumpkin is baking sauté the pork sausage in a skillet until brown. Drain well.

6. Heat the oil in the same pan, and sauté the celery and onion until tender. Add the mushrooms and cook 2 minutes more.

7. Mix together the egg, sour cream, and Parmesan cheese, and combine with the sausage mixture. Spoon into the pumpkin halves.

8. Bake, uncovered, for 25 minutes.

9. Cut each half into 2 servings. Garnish with parsley.

YIELD: 4 SERVINGS

Pumpkin Pancakes

The "Pumpkin Capital of the World" is Morton, Illinois, home of Libby's pumpkin cannery and host of the annual Morton Pumpkin Festival, held each September since 1967. At the festival you can sample pumpkin pancakes for breakfast, pumpkin chili for lunch, and pumpkin pie and ice cream for dessert. At one time, Libby's published the Great Pumpkin Cookbook, *from which this recipe was adapted. When I'm cooking for a gang, I double the ingredients and spread the batter evenly into a 15 by 10-inch jelly roll pan, bake it at 425°F (220°C) for 15 minutes, and cut it into squares.*

1 cup flour	¼ cup pumpkin puree
1 tablespoon brown sugar	1 small egg
½ teaspoon baking powder	1 tablespoon vegetable oil
½ teaspoon salt	1 apple, peeled, cored, and
¾ cup milk	sliced thin

1. In one bowl, combine the dry ingredients.

2. In a second bowl, combine the milk, pumpkin, egg, and oil. Stir together the dry ingredients, just to moisten. Add the apple slices.

3. Warm your griddle to 375°F (190°C), hot enough to make a drop of water sizzle. For each pancake, spread ¼ cup (133 ml) of batter into a 4-inch (10 cm) circle. Cook until the surface looks dry, then turn and cook 2 to 3 minutes more.

4. Serve with maple syrup or cranberry sauce.

YIELD: **8** PANCAKES

Pumpkin Brioche

When culinary professional Candy Schermerhorn of Peoria, Arizona, cooks with pumpkin, she uses only the finest spices, which she insists must come from The Spice House of Milwaukee, Wisconsin. "The opulent flavor of this wonderful aromatic bread," says Candy, "comes from combining fine spices with pumpkin and the rich malty essence of a bock beer. Serve this brioche toasted, with whipped honey butter and oolong tea for an elegant breakfast, or fill it with curried chicken salad for a memorable repast." Candy recommends using pumpkin spice beer when you have it (the recipe appears later in this chapter), or a bock or doppel bock beer. For added flavor and texture, you may include ⅔ cup of toasted, finely chopped pecans.

Dough

- ½ cup bock beer
- 1 tablespoon bread yeast
- 5½–6 cups bread flour, divided
- 2 pieces candied ginger, chopped coarsely
- 2 teaspoons orange zest, minced finely
- ½ cup brown sugar
- 1¼ cups pumpkin puree
- 7 tablespoons butter
- 2 large eggs
- 2 teaspoons salt
- 2 teaspoons Chinese 5-spice
- 1 teaspoon ground coriander
- ¼ teaspoon ground cardamom

Glaze

- 1 small egg white
- 1 tablespoon honey

1. Heat the beer to 100°F (38°C). In a large bowl, whisk it with the yeast and 1 tablespoon of the bread flour. Set aside for 15 to 20 minutes.
2. In a blender, incorporate the ginger and zest with the brown sugar.
3. Stir the sugar mixture into the yeast mixture. Add 2 more cups of flour, along with the rest of the dough ingredients.
4. Continue stirring in the remaining flour — just enough to make the dough pull away from the bowl. Turn the dough onto a lightly floured surface and knead for 10 minutes, adding only enough flour to keep it from sticking. When the dough is smooth and elastic, place it in a lightly oiled bowl. Cover and let rise in a warm spot until doubled.
5. Punch down the dough. Divide it in half to make 2 loaves, or into 12 pieces to make individual rolls. Form into your desired shape (Candy's favorite is a large braid), place in generously buttered pans, cover, and let rise until doubled.
6. Preheat your oven to 350°F (175°C).
7. Beat together the egg white and honey to make the glaze. Brush generously over the tops of the breads. Bake until the tops are deep gold and bottoms are well browned.

YIELD: 2 LOAVES OR 12 ROLLS

Pumpkin Soup

*This unique soup recipe was developed by Candy Schermerhorn —
teacher, author of the* Great American Beer Cookbook *(Brewers
Publications), and TV cooking personality on NBC's affiliate in
Phoenix, Arizona. For this soup, Candy recommends using any full-
bodied beer that doesn't have a high hop content (in other words, isn't
extremely bitter). The recipe requires some advance preparation,
including making the chicken or vegetable stock by simmering a rich
chicken or vegetable broth down to half its original volume. You'll also
need to bake the onion and garlic, and toast the nuts: Bake the
unpeeled onion in a microwave oven for about 6 minutes on high,
until it's softened like a baked potato; or bake it in a conventional oven
at 350°F (175°C) for 40 minutes. Bake the unpeeled garlic and roast
the nuts on a cookie sheet in a 350°F (175°C) oven for 15 minutes.
Cool the onion and garlic thoroughly before peeling them.*

1 medium yellow onion, baked	2 cups chicken or vegetable stock
6 cloves garlic, baked	1½ cups pumpkin puree
⅔ cup pecans or walnuts, toasted	1 cup sour cream
¼ teaspoon ginger	1 extra-large egg
¼ teaspoon allspice	½ cup milk
1 cup amber lager	salt and pepper

1. In a food processor, combine the onion, garlic, nuts, and spices. Process fairly smooth.
2. Heat together the lager, stock, and pumpkin. Stir in the pureed mixture. Simmer 15 minutes.
3. Stir in the sour cream.
4. Beat together the egg and milk. Stirring constantly, pour slowly into the soup. Without boiling, heat 10 minutes more.
5. Season to taste with salt and pepper. Serve hot.

YIELD: 6 SERVINGS

Pumpkin-Tomato Soup with Basil

Years ago, Mary Joan Barrett of Mallorytown, Ontario, became enchanted with fields of pumpkins growing on a friend's farm. "When, in appreciation of my enthusiasm," says Joan, "my friend filled the trunk of my car with golden globes, I wondered how I could cook them and bake them and, most important, preserve them so I wouldn't have to throw any of them out." She tested "odds and ends of recipes found here and there" and compiled the best formulas into a delightful cookbook, In Praise of Pumpkins *(History Unlimited). "I love homemade soup,"* Joan enthuses, and this soup has become a Barrett family favorite.*

I small pumpkin, peeled, seeded, and cut into I" (2.5 cm) cubes	I teaspoon salt freshly ground pepper to taste
8 carrots, sliced	I teaspoon sugar
4 cups chicken stock	¼ cup cream
¼ cup butter	2 tablespoons basil, chopped
I medium onion, chopped	
I cup mushrooms, sliced	12 stuffed green olives, sliced
6 medium tomatoes, skinned and chopped	

I. In a large soup pot, combine the pumpkin cubes, carrot slices, and chicken stock. Bring to a boil. Simmer for 30 minutes.

2. In a separate saucepan, melt the butter and in it sauté the onion and mushrooms until golden brown.

3. Add the tomatoes. Stir-fry for 5 minutes; remove from heat.

4. In small batches, puree the pumpkin mixture and sautéed vegetables in a food processor. Return to the soup pot.

5. Combine the salt, pepper, sugar, and cream. Add to the pot.

6. Add the chopped basil. Let stand on low heat for 5 minutes.

7. Divide the soup among 4 to 6 bowls. Garnish each with sliced olives.

YIELD: 4–6 SERVINGS

Pumpkin Dinner Rolls

In researching her book In Praise of Pumpkins, *historian Mary Joan Barrett became curious about the folklore associated with pumpkins, and couldn't help including a few tidbits in her book. "When I came across an old legend that, on Halloween, all the pumpkins leave their vines and dance across the fields," she says, "I was truly hooked on pumpkins." The Barrett family is now hooked on these unusual and delicious dinner rolls.*

I packet yeast	½ cup vegetable oil
I tablespoon maple syrup	6¾ cups flour
½ cup lukewarm water	I teaspoon salt
I cup milk, scalded and cooled	I teaspoon ginger
I cup pumpkin puree	½ teaspoon cinnamon
I cup brown sugar	½ teaspoon nutmeg

1. In a large bowl, combine the yeast, syrup, and water. Set aside for 15 minutes.
2. In a medium bowl, combine the milk, pumpkin, sugar, and oil.
3. Into yeast, stir the pumpkin mixture alternately with the flour. Add the remaining ingredients.
4. Mix until a soft dough forms. Transfer the dough to a floured pastry board. Knead until smooth and elastic, about 10 minutes. Place the dough in large greased bowl, cover with a towel, and let rise in a warm, draft-free place until doubled in volume, about 2½ hours.
5. Turn the dough onto a floured board and punch down, kneading slightly. Let it rest for 30 minutes. Roll out to about 1 inch (2.5 cm) thick. Dip your biscuit cutter into flour before cutting each roll. Arrange rolls close together on greased baking sheets. Cover and let rise until doubled in volume, about 1 hour.
6. Preheat your oven to 350°F (175°C). Bake the rolls for 25 minutes, or until the tops sound hollow when tapped.

YIELD: 4 DOZEN ROLLS

Pumpkin Butter

What better treat to serve on pumpkin dinner rolls than pumpkin but-ter like this, from Vala's Pumpkin Patch Fall Fun Cookbook? *Increase the amounts of ingredients as necessary to accommodate whatever quantity of pumpkin you wish to make into butter. Feel free to add all-spice, cloves, or your other favorite spices. If you substitute brown sugar for sugar and double the spices, your pumpkin butter will taste much like traditional apple butter. For sugar-free pumpkin butter, stew pumpkin meat in apple juice concentrate (from the frozen juice depart-ment of any grocery store). As a low-acid food, pumpkin butter is not safe for water bath canning. It will keep for several weeks in the refrig-erator or several months in the freezer.*

3 cups pumpkin puree
I cup sugar
½ teaspoon cinnamon
¼ teaspoon nutmeg

I. Combine all ingredients in a saucepan. Cook until thick, stirring often to prevent scorching.
2. Pour into hot sterilized jars and seal.

YIELD: 3 HALF-PINT JARS

Hollis's Pumpkin Chips

*Not all varieties of pumpkin have the right texture to make good pre-
serves — which should consist of firm pumpkin slices, not pumpkin
mush. While I always get nice firm preserves when I use old-fashioned
Sugar varieties, one year I was surprised by a volunteer pumpkin of
unknown origin that made the best chips ever. Spread these mar-
maladelike preserves on English muffins or breakfast toast, serve them
with hot dinner rolls, or delight the peanut-butter-and-jelly crowd by
using pumpkin chips in place of grape jelly. This recipe was given to me
in northern California by the late Hollis Gibson — an imaginative
cook, dear lady, and expert pumpkin grower.*

> 4¼ pounds pumpkin slices, each about
>   ¼" x 1" x 2"
> 6⅓ cups sugar
> 2 lemons, sliced thin
> 1 orange, sliced thin
>   pinch salt

1. Combine the pumpkin slices and sugar. Let stand overnight.
2. Drain, saving liquid.
3. Boil liquid to 230°F (110°C), about 25 minutes.
4. Add the pumpkin, lemon, and orange slices, along with the salt.
   Cook until the liquid turns clear and the pumpkin becomes
   transparent, about 2 hours.
5. Fill 7 ½-pint canning jars, leaving ¼-inch (6 mm) headspace.
6. Process for 5 minutes in enough boiling water to cover the jars.
   Begin timing when water returns to a boil.

YIELD: 7 HALF-PINT JARS

Fried Pumpkin Blossoms

Fried pumpkin blossoms come in many forms. The flowers may be chopped and stirred into fritter batter. Whole blossoms may be stuffed with cheese, perhaps mixed with vegetables such as corn and chopped tomatoes, then dipped in batter and deep-fried. Or plain blossoms may be battered and fried. This basic recipe comes from Lin Ayers of the Pumpkin Patch in Santa Paula, California.

24 pumpkin blossoms
2 eggs
⅓ cup milk
1 tablespoon parsley

½ teaspoon salt
⅛ teaspoon pepper
⅔ cup yellow cornmeal
oil or butter

1. Wash pumpkin blossoms and remove the centers.
2. Beat together the eggs, milk, parsley, salt, and pepper.
3. Dip blossoms one at a time in this mixture, then roll them in the cornmeal.
4. Fry briefly on both sides in oil or butter until golden brown.
5. Serve warm.

YIELD: **8** SERVINGS

Culinary Pumpkin Blossoms

When pumpkin blossoms start to form, use them to garnish salads or add them to soups and stews. You might plant extra vines just for their blossoms, or wait to pick flowers until an adequate number of fruits have set on each vine. While the fruits are setting, you can pick a few (no more) male flowers without interfering with pollination.

Pick blossoms early in the morning, selecting those that have just opened so they can be rinsed easily. Keep the flowers fresh by placing them in ice water in the refrigerator until you're ready to use them. The flavor and texture of some blossoms is better than others, so choose which vines to harvest by taste-testing a flower or two first.

Pumpkin Pickles

These sweet pickles make a spicy and festive addition to any holiday table. They go especially well with goose, duck, or pork roast. The recipe works best with a pumpkin variety that remains firm even after it has been lightly steamed. Many varieties turn mealy, giving the pickles an unpleasant texture. My best pickles come from old-fashioned Sugar pumpkins. For easy removal of the spices at the end, pack them in a large tea ball. If you leave the spices in the jars, they'll discolor your pickles.

2 medium pie pumpkins, cut, cored, peeled, and diced (about 7 cups pumpkin cubes)	2 sticks cinnamon 15 cloves 2⅓ cups 4% vinegar 2⅓ cups sugar

1. Steam the pumpkin cubes until just tender, about 10 minutes. Drain.

2. Put the spices in a tea ball. Simmer them with the vinegar and sugar for 15 minutes.

3. Simmer the pumpkin cubes in this syrup for 3 minutes. Set aside for 24 hours.

4. Start water boiling in a canner. Heat the pumpkin/syrup mix and simmer for 5 minutes. Remove the spices and pack into 7 ½-pint jars, leaving ½-inch (12 mm) headspace.

5. Process in a boiling water bath for 5 minutes, counting from when the water returns to a full boil.

YIELD: 7 HALF-PINT JARS

166 ◆ THE PERFECT PUMPKIN

Pumpkin Muffins

This is the kind of recipe I love — it's easy to make, showcases the flavor of pumpkin, and is versatile (see box below).

½ cup butter
¾ cup brown sugar
¼ cup honey
1 egg
1 cup pumpkin puree

1½ cups flour
1 teaspoon baking soda
¼ teaspoon salt
½ cup chopped nuts
(pecans or walnuts)

1. Preheat oven to 400°F (205°C).

2. Cream the butter. Gradually beat in the sugar.

3. Add the honey, egg, and pumpkin, mixing well.

4. Combine the dry ingredients and add to the pumpkin mixture. Stir in the nuts.

5. Fill greased muffin tins three-quarters full. Bake for 18 minutes.

YIELD: 18 MUFFINS

Versatile Variations

For a stronger "harvest" flavor	Substitute molasses for honey
For a traditional spicy flavor	Add 1 teaspoon cinnamon or pumpkin pie spice
For earthiness	Use pumpkin seeds instead of nuts
For elegance	Add the grated rind of 1 orange
For fruitiness	Stir in ½ cup raisins, chopped prunes, or chopped dried apricots
For political correctness	Add both fruit and ½ cup oat or wheat bran

Pumpcan Bread

Here's another recipe from my dear friend Hollis Gibson, who got a kick out of its punny name. This scrumptious, not-too-sweet bread is baked in small coffee cans, providing ready-made gift containers. When the bread has cooled, seal each can with its plastic lid, wrap the can with colorful paper, and add a bow. If you're feeling especially creative, use orange construction paper to make a pumpkin-shaped gift tag.

3 cups flour	2 eggs, beaten
1 teaspoon baking powder	1 cup milk
1 teaspoon salt	1 cup pumpkin puree
1 teaspoon cinnamon	½ cup brown sugar
½ teaspoon nutmeg	¼ cup vegetable oil
¼ teaspoon cloves	1 teaspoon baking soda
1 cup chopped nuts	

1. Preheat oven to 350°F (175°C).

2. Mix the dry ingredients.

3. In a separate bowl, combine the moist ingredients. Blend them into the dry mixture.

4. Divide the batter into 2 clean, greased 13-ounce coffee cans. Bake for 1 hour and 15 minutes.

YIELD: 2 LOAVES

Canned Pumpkin Bread

This bread is baked in a canning jar where, as long as the seal isn't broken, it will last forever. The bread makes wonderful gifts, as well as a fine addition to the well-stocked pantry. The recipe was developed by Gerald Kuhn (now retired), professor of food science at Pennsylvania State University, and his colleagues, whose work was supported by the U.S. Department of Agriculture. This is one recipe you don't want to modify, warns Dr. Kuhn, as its moisture content has been adjusted to make it perfectly safe for preserving in jars. To bake this bread, you'll need 8 1-pint, wide-mouthed glass canning jars with 2-piece lids.

⅔ cup shortening
2⅔ cups sugar
4 eggs
2 cups pumpkin puree
⅔ cup water
3⅓ cups flour
½ teaspoon baking powder

2 teaspoon baking soda
1½ teaspoons salt
1 teaspoon cinnamon
1 teaspoon ground cloves
⅔ cup chopped nuts (optional)

1. Preheat oven to 325°F (160°C).

2. Cream together the shortening and sugar.

3. Beat in the eggs, pumpkin, and water.

4. Sift together the dry ingredients. Add to the pumpkin mixture, along with the nuts, if desired.

5. Pour the batter into clean, greased canning jars, filling them half full. Bake in jars *without lids* for about 25 minutes, or until the bread rises and pulls away from the sides of the jars.

6. When the bread is done, remove 1 jar at a time from the oven, clean its rim, and firmly screw on a 2-piece canning lid. Let the jars cool on the counter away from drafts. You can tell each jar has become vacuum-sealed when its dome is sucked downward at the center during cooling. Store jars in a cool, dry, dark place.

YIELD: **8** ONE-PINT JARS

Swiss-Style Pumpkin

The highlight of the year at Stonycreek Farm in Noblesville, Indiana, is October's monthlong Pumpkin Harvest Festival. Folks come from miles around to ride a hay wagon into the fields and choose from among 60,000 pumpkins. If owners Loren and Barbara Schmierer know you plan to cook your pumpkin, they'll point you toward the Sugar pumpkins and share recipes like this one.

3 cups raw pumpkin, sliced
⅓ cup butter
2 eggs, beaten
¼ cup milk
1 teaspoon salt
dash cayenne
¼ teaspoon dry mustard
½ cup shredded Swiss cheese
Parmesan cheese

1. Sauté the pumpkin in the butter until tender. Remove to a serving dish.
2. In remaining liquid in pan, combine the eggs, milk, spices, and Swiss cheese. Heat until the cheese melts.
3. Pour the cheese mix over pumpkin. Top with Parmesan.

YIELD: 6 SERVINGS

Traditional Pumpkin Pie

Of all the pumpkin pies I've tasted over the years, this one is my absolute favorite. Sometimes I substitute 2 tablespoons bourbon or dark rum for the boiling water. Sometimes I make pumpkin pudding by baking the filling in individual serving bowls or in the hollowed-out shells of baby pumpkins. Whether I make pudding or pie, I heap each serving with whipped cream (perhaps garnished with bits of grated or finely chopped candied ginger), vanilla ice cream, or rum raisin ice cream.

2 eggs
¾ cup brown sugar
5 ounces evaporated milk
1½ teaspoons cinnamon
½ teaspoon salt
½ teaspoon ginger

¼ teaspoon nutmeg
2 tablespoons boiling water
1½ cups scorched pumpkin
¼ cup half and half
1 prepared, unbaked 9" pastry shell

1. Preheat oven to 425°F (220°C).

2. Beat the eggs and add the sugar, milk, spices, and boiling water.

3. Combine with the pumpkin and half and half.

4. Pour into the pastry shell. Bake in the preheated oven for 15 minutes, then lower the heat to 300°F (150°C) and bake for 25 minutes more, or until the filling completely coagulates except for a small circle at the center.

YIELD: ONE 9" PIE

The Most Pies

"The most pies ever made from one of our pumpkins was 442, which were sold for $3 each to help fund a local senior citizen home," says Howard Dill, developer of 'Dill's Atlantic Giant' pumpkin.

Double Ginger Pumpkin Pie
with Bourbon

Marcia Adams — cookbook author and producer of the PBS TV series Marcia Adams' Kitchen — *and I met when we were both speakers at the annual Farm Progress Show. We have kept in touch and I follow her seasonal activities through her quarterly newsletter, "Heartland Journal." Marcia spends many happy hours in her garden, then brings the fruits of her labors into her kitchen to create such delights as this flavorful pie, which she tops with sweetened whipped cream and serves as dessert following the first chili supper of the fall season.*

Ginger-nut layer
- 2 tablespoons butter, softened
- ¼ cup brown sugar
- 3 tablespoons candied ginger, chopped fine
- ¼ cup black walnuts
- 1 prepared, unbaked 9" pastry shell

Filling
- 2 large eggs
- 1 cup light brown sugar
- 2 cups pumpkin puree
- 1 teaspoon ginger
- ½ teaspoon cinnamon
- ½ teaspoon allspice
- ¼ teaspoon mace
- ¼ teaspoon nutmeg
- ¼ teaspoon salt
- 1 cup evaporated milk
- 2 tablespoons bourbon
- 1 teaspoon vanilla extract

1. Preheat oven to 400°F (205°C).

2. *For the ginger-nut layer:* In small bowl, combine the butter and sugar. Add the ginger and nuts. Blend until crumbly.

3. Pierce the pie shell with a fork. Gently press the ginger mixture into the bottom of the shell. Bake for 10 minutes, or until bubbly and golden brown. Remove from the oven and set aside.

4. *For the filling:* Reduce oven to 350°F (175°C).

5. Beat together the eggs and sugar. Add the pumpkin and spices, blending well.

6. Add the milk, bourbon, and vanilla. Beat slowly until the filling is just combined and smooth. Pour into the shell.

7. Bake for 40 minutes, or until a table knife inserted toward the edge comes out clean. The center should be moist, since the pie continues cooking as it cools.

YIELD: **6–8** SERVINGS

Pumpkin Pie Spice

A recipe calling for pumpkin pie spice refers to a blend of spices traditionally associated with pumpkin pie: cinnamon, ginger, nutmeg, and sometimes cloves. You can buy pumpkin pie spice at the grocery, or you can create your own unique blend, adjusting the amounts of each spice until the flavor tickles your taste buds. To get the most from your spices, buy the whole dried kind and grind them yourself. Store your spice blend in an airtight jar. Here, to get you started, are three popular formulas:

	(1)	(2)	(3)
Cinnamon	¼ cup	¼ cup	¼ cup
Ginger	4 teaspoons	1 tablespoon	2 tablespoons
Nutmeg	2 teaspoons	1 tablespoon	1 tablespoon
Cloves	—	1 tablespoon	1 tablespoon

Pumpkin Torte

I've been making pumpkin torte since long before I started keeping track of where my recipes come from. It's really not a torte, but who am I to change the name of this fine recipe, which tastes suspiciously like pumpkin pie? I'll bet the person who created this treat pressed sugar crust dough into a square pan instead of a pie tin, then poured in the filling. Whatever its origin, pumpkin torte is so delicious that it doesn't last long at our house.

Crust

- 1 cup sifted flour
- ¼ cup brown sugar
- ⅓ cup butter
- ½ cup walnuts, chopped fine

Filling

- 3 ounces cream cheese, softened
- 1 egg
- 2 cups pumpkin puree
- 14 ounces sweetened condensed milk
- ½ teaspoon cinnamon
- ⅛ teaspoon nutmeg
- ⅛ teaspoon cloves
- ⅛ teaspoon ginger
- 1 cup hot water
- 16 walnut halves

1. Preheat oven to 350°F (175°C).
2. *For the crust:* Combine the flour and sugar. Cut in the butter. Add the nuts.
3. Press into an 8 by 8-inch pan. Bake for 20 minutes, or until brown.
4. *For the filling:* With the oven still heated to 350°F (175°C), beat the cream cheese with the egg. Add the pumpkin, milk, and spices. Beat until smooth. Stir in the hot water.
5. Pour into the baked crust. Garnish with the walnut halves.
6. Bake for 50 minutes, or until firm.
7. Cool. Cut into 16 squares, each with a walnut half in the center.

YIELD: 16 SERVINGS

Pumpkin Cheesecake

Lin Ayers of the Pumpkin Patch in Santa Paula, California, collected recipes from "family members, friends, neighbors, strangers, magazines, and newspapers" and put them together into a ring-bound packet to distribute to customers who ask "How do you cook pumpkin?" Here's one of Lin's favorites.

Crust
- ⅓ cup margarine
- ⅓ cup sugar
- 1 egg
- 1¼ cups flour

Filling
- 20 ounces crushed pineapple
- ¾ cup pineapple juice
- 2 cups pumpkin puree
- 1 cup brown sugar
- 3 eggs, beaten
- 1 teaspoon cinnamon
- ½ teaspoon ginger
- 1 envelope unflavored gelatin
- 16 ounces cream cheese, softened
- 1 tablespoon vanilla

Topping
- ½ cup whipping cream

1. Preheat oven to 400°F (205°C).

2. *For the crust:* Cream together the margarine and sugar. Blend in the egg. Add the flour and mix well.

3. Press the dough into the bottom and sides of a 10-inch pie pan. Bake for 5 minutes. Remove from the oven and set aside.

4. *For the filling:* Drain the crushed pineapple, saving the juice. Cover the pineapple and refrigerate. (You'll use it later, for the topping; see step 8.)

5. In a saucepan, combine ¾ cup of the reserved pineapple juice with the pumpkin, sugar, eggs, spices, and gelatin. Cover and simmer gently, stirring occasionally for 30 minutes.

6. Beat together the softened cream cheese and vanilla until fluffy. Gradually beat in the warm pumpkin mixture until well blended.

7. Pour into the prepared crust. Cover and refrigerate overnight.
8. *For the topping:* When you're ready to serve, whip the cream and fold in the reserved pineapple. Spoon the topping onto the cheesecake.

YIELD: **8** SERVINGS

Pumpkin Cake

This recipe has been in our family for a number of years and has become a fall favorite. Dates give the cake a fruitcakelike quality, but there's no reason you couldn't substitute raisins or chopped prunes, if they're closer at hand. The cake slices best when made a day ahead, or at least cooled in the refrigerator for a few hours.

1 cup brown sugar	½ teaspoon salt
⅓ cup shortening	¼ teaspoon nutmeg
2 eggs	¼ teaspoon ginger
1 cup pumpkin puree	¼ teaspoon cloves
2 cups flour	¼ teaspoon baking soda
2 teaspoons baking powder	¼ cup milk
1 teaspoon cinnamon	1 cup chopped walnuts

1. Preheat oven to 325°F (165°C).
2. Cream together the sugar, shortening, eggs and pumpkin. Sift the dry ingredients together in a separate bowl.
3. Add the flour mixture to the creamed mixture in alternating portions with the milk. Beat well. Add the walnuts and dates.
4. Bake in a greased standard-size loaf pan for 1 hour.

YIELD: **1** LOAF

Pumpkin Cupcakes

Old-order Amish bishop Henry E. Mast put a notice in his church bulletin asking the ladies of Holmes and Wayne Counties, Ohio, to send him their favorite recipes, which he compiled into a cookbook. First printed on the bishop's home press in 1986, Cooking with the Horse & Buggy People *(Carlisle Printing) has become a classic. Mrs. Reuben Miller contributed this recipe for pumpkin cupcakes.*

Cupcakes
- 2 cups sugar
- 2 cups pumpkin puree
- 4 eggs, beaten
- 1 cup vegetable oil
- 2 cups flour
- 2 teaspoons baking soda
- 2 teaspoons baking powder
- 2 teaspoons cinnamon

- 1 teaspoon nutmeg
- 1 teaspoon Pumpkin Pie Spice (page 173)
- ½ teaspoon salt

Frosting
- 3 cups powdered sugar
- ½ cup margarine, softened
- 1 ounce cream cheese

1. Preheat oven to 350°F (175°C).

2. Beat together the sugar, pumpkin, eggs, and oil. Stir together the remaining ingredients and blend them in.

3. Fill 24 cupcake cups with batter. Bake for 30 minutes. Cool.

4. Combine frosting ingredients and frost cupcakes when cool.

YIELD: **24** CUPCAKES

Pumpkin Substitutes

If you're looking for new ways to prepare pumpkin, try using a thick puree in any recipe calling for mashed sweet potatoes or winter squash. By the same token, if you run short of pumpkin to prepare your favorite recipe, you may substitute mashed cooked sweet potatoes or any winter squash of similar consistency, but don't expect a pumpkin flavor. Commercially canned pumpkin is not a satisfactory substitute for fresh or home-canned Sugar pumpkin, but has the advantage of being available year-around.

Pumpkin Cookies

These light, cake-type cookies may be made in two ways. If you plan to serve them to adults, make smaller cookies and dust them with powdered sugar. For the younger set, make larger mounds and sandwich two together with frosting, creating a unique roundish, bright orange treat kids love. In either case, these cookies taste best after they've aged for at least a day. Since we don't always have prunes in the house, I'm likely to substitute currants or raisins.

Cookies

- ½ cup butter, softened
- 1 cup sugar
- 2 large eggs
- 2 teaspoons vanilla
- 1 cup pumpkin puree
- 4 teaspoons baking powder
- ½ teaspoon nutmeg
- ¼ teaspoon salt
- 2½ cups flour, divided
- 1½ cups chopped prunes
- ½ cup chopped walnuts

Frosting (optional)

- 3 ounces cream cheese, softened
- 1½ cups powdered sugar
- 1 teaspoon vanilla

1. Preheat oven to 375°F (190°C).
2. In a large bowl, beat the butter with the sugar until fluffy. Add the eggs, vanilla, pumpkin, baking powder, spices, and 1 cup of the flour.
3. Gradually beat in the remaining 1½ cups of flour. Stir the prunes and walnuts into the stiff dough.
4. Drop the cookie dough by scant or heaping tablespoonfuls onto a greased cookie sheet. Bake for 12 to 15 minutes, or until the bottoms are lightly browned.
5. Cool on wire racks. Dust cookies with powdered sugar *or* sandwich two together with a scant teaspoonful of frosting between them.

YIELD: ABOUT 7 DOZEN SMALL COOKIES OR
3 DOZEN SANDWICH COOKIES

Pumpkin Ice Cream Roll

A big hit at the annual Pumpkin Show in McEwen, Tennessee, is Gail Wright's pumpkin ice cream roll. Gail wouldn't part with her special recipe, which she developed as a result of a "happy accident." So I was delighted when my mother brought a similar recipe home from a visit with friends in the Southwest. To roll the cake, you'll need a clean linen tea towel or nonterry cotton dish towel. After sprinkling the towel with sifted powdered sugar to keep the cake from sticking, roll the cake and towel together, lengthwise. Let the cake cool, seam side down, then unroll it and spread the filling. Use any ice cream flavor you feel is compatible with pumpkin — vanilla, rum raisin, maple, pumpkin (homemade from the recipe that follows) — or orange sherbet. Serve each slice of frozen cake with a spoonful of warmed cranberry sauce.

3 eggs
I cup sugar
⅔ cup pumpkin puree
I teaspoon baking soda
½ teaspoon cinnamon

¾ cup flour
½ cup finely chopped nuts
  sifted powdered sugar
I quart ice cream, softened

I. Preheat oven to 375°F (190°C).

2. Combine the first 6 ingredients and mix well.

3. Pour into a greased 15 by 10-inch jelly roll pan, lined with greased waxed paper. Sprinkle with the nuts. Bake 15 to 17 minutes.

4. Sprinkle sifted powdered sugar onto a tea towel. Turn the cake on to the towel, pull off the waxed paper and roll the cake while hot.

5. Cool for 1½ to 2 hours.

6. Unroll the cake and spread with the ice cream.

7. Reroll and seal in plastic wrap, then aluminum foil. Freeze.

YIELD: 10–12 SERVINGS

Pumpkin Ice Cream with Cranberry-Raspberry Sauce

Marcia Adams of Fort Wayne, Indiana, first enjoyed this unusual dessert at the Checkerberry Inn in Goshen, Indiana. "I came right home," says Marcia, "and worked up this recipe, using the scanty instructions given to me by the chef. It is the ultimate winter holiday dessert — eat small portions without guilt."

Ice cream
- 15 egg yolks
- 1½ cups sugar
- 2 teaspoons vanilla
- ¼ teaspoon salt
- 1 tablespoon Pumpkin Pie Spice (page 173)
- 1 quart half and half
- 1 cup whipping cream
- 3½ cups pumpkin puree
- 1 tablespoon bitters

Sauce
- ½ cup water
- 1 cup sugar
- 12 ounces cranberries, sorted and rinsed
- 12 ounces red raspberry preserves
- 2 tablespoons Triple Sec

1. *For the ice cream:* In a large, heavy saucepan whisk the egg yolks, sugar, vanilla, and spices. Whisk in the half and half and cream.

2. Cook over medium-low heat, stirring with a wooden spoon, about 20 minutes, or until the mixture thickens and just begins to bubble at the center.

3. Remove from the heat and whisk in the pumpkin and bitters.

4. Cover and refrigerate overnight. Process in an ice cream maker according to the manufacturer's instructions. Harden in the freezer for at least 2 hours.

5. *For the sauce:* In a medium saucepan, combine the water and sugar.

6. Bring to a boil and add the cranberries. Return to a boil, reduce heat, and cook gently, uncovered, 10 minutes, stirring occasionally.

7. Remove from the heat and stir in the preserves.

8. Cool completely and add the Triple Sec.

YIELD: 12–16 SERVINGS

Pumpkin Fudge

I was immediately intrigued when I discovered pumpkin fudge at a local gift shop, but disappointed to learn it had been made from a mix. Pumpkin-stand owners tell me their most often requested recipe is that for fudge. Jan Vala of Vala's Pumpkin Patch in Gretna, Nebraska, and Barbara Schmierer of Stonycreek Farm in Noblesville, Indiana, both sent me the from-scratch recipe. The first time I made it, I mistakenly used ¾ cup sugar instead of 3 cups and cooked the mixture for only 10 minutes. The "fudge" came out the consistency of a spread — so we served it like jam and found it to be outrageously delicious. The fudge, properly made, is pretty good too.

3 cups sugar
¾ cup butter
1 can (5 ounces) evaporated milk
½ cup pumpkin puree
1 teaspoon Pumpkin Pie Spice (page 173)

12 ounces butterscotch bits
7 ounces marshmallow creme
1 cup chopped nuts (walnut or pecans)
1 teaspoon vanilla

1. In a large, heavy saucepan, combine the first 5 ingredients. Stirring constantly, bring to a boil, then reduce the heat and cook to the soft-ball stage (234°F, 115°C), about 25 minutes.
2. Remove from heat and stir in the butterscotch bits. Add the remaining ingredients.
3. Blend well and spread evenly in a buttered 13 by 9-inch pan.
4. Cool and cut into squares. Wrap tightly and store in the refrigerator.

YIELD: 3¼ POUNDS

Pumpkin Beer

The American Philosophical Society published this recipe for pumpkin ale in February 1771: "Let the Pompion be beaten in a Trough and pressed as Apples. The expressed Juice is to be boiled in a Copper a considerable Time and carefully skimmed that there may be no Remains of the fibrous Part of the Pulp. After that Intention is answered let the Liquor be hopped, cooled, fermented &c. as Malt Beer." The anonymous author noted that the ale had a slight "twang," which mellowed after two years in the bottle.

I've long heard rumors about delicious pumpkin beer, but for some time every recipe I ran across either contained so many other ingredients that the pumpkin became incidental, or produced a vile-tasting beer (or both). I guess I'm not alone. In the Fall 1994 issue of the homebrewer's magazine *Zymurgy,* physicist Alan Barnes of Nashville, Tennessee, wrote a tale of woe about trying to make pumpkin ale. Alan was asking for trouble from the start, I noted from his story, by using a 13-pound (5.9 kg) jack-o'-lantern type pumpkin instead of smaller Sugar pumpkins. But that wasn't the only problem. "The aroma was terrible," says Alan of his brew, "and the flavor was harsh with an overpowering nutmeg/mace element."

Indeed, James Spence of the American Homebrewers Association in Boulder, Colorado, told me that "the main emphasis in pumpkin recipes seems to be on creating a pumpkin *pie* beer." If you already have a favorite recipe for a pale, lightly hopped ale, you have the foundation for a fine pumpkin beer. In addition to your regular recipe, for 5 gallons of beer you'll need 5 pounds of pumpkin meat, cut into small squares, plus 1½ teaspoons of pumpkin pie spice. While your malt and hops boil, add the pumpkin chunks about halfway through the hour, and add the spices for the last 15 minutes. When your boiling time is up, remove the pumpkin when you remove the hops, and continue with your recipe as you normally would.

If you haven't made beer before, you'll need a 7-gallon fermenter and a 5-gallon carboy, which is basically a large bottle of the sort used for water coolers. The fermenter allows plenty of room for the brew to bubble, while the carboy minimizes the amount of oxygen that comes into contact with the brew's surface. Fermenters and carboys, and the air locks required to seal them, are available from home beer- and wine-making suppliers, as are malt extract, hops, yeast, Irish moss (to keep your beer from being cloudy), a siphon (for racking — the process of siphoning clear liquid off bottom sediment), reusable beer bottles, and a capper. A hydrometer also comes in handy for measuring the brew's sugar content, so your bottles won't blow up because you bottled your brew before it finished fermenting. At bottling time, use corn sugar (*not* cane sugar) to give your beer a good head when you pour it into the glass.

Skinny Puppy Pumpkin Ale

The recipe for this robust beer was created by David Ruggiero, owner of the homebrew supply shop Barleymalt & Vine in Newton, Massachusetts. "The beer was named by a friend," says David. "I had a thin dog and I thought he was referring to my pup, but he later told me it's the name of a punk rock group." David got interested in brewing with pumpkins after reading about the use of native ingredients in the beers of old New England. "It should be obvious," says David, "that you are drinking a liq-uid, alcoholic, pumpkin pie." If you don't agree, reduce the amount of spices or leave them out. Microbrewer Russ Kness of Albia, Iowa, brewed this ale using 1 teaspoon pumpkin pie spice and it tasted great. For bit-tering hops use Cascade, Mt. Hood, or Willammette, and for ale yeast use either Munton & Fisson or Edme.

7 pounds amber malt extract	1 teaspoon cinnamon
2 gallons boiling water	½ teaspoon ginger
1 ounce bittering hops	¼ teaspoon nutmeg
½ teaspoon Irish moss	7 grams ale yeast
4 pounds pumpkin, in 1" (2.5 cm) cubes	1 cup water
	corn sugar

1. Dissolve the malt extract in the boiling water. Stir until a boil is reestablished.
2. Add the bittering hops and boil for 60 minutes.
3. After 40 minutes, add the Irish moss.
4. After 55 minutes, add the pumpkin and spices.

5. Combine the ale yeast and 1 cup of water. Set aside.
6. Transfer the pumpkin to a fermenter. Cool the liquid and strain into the fermenter to remove the hops. Fill the fermenter to 5 gallons with boiled, cooled water.
7. When the temperature falls below 75°F (24°C), stir in the dissolved yeast. Starting gravity (as determined by a hydrometer) is 1.045 to 1.048.
8. When fermentation stops, rack the beer into a carboy, straining out the pumpkin and taking care not to stir up the bottom sediment.
9. Rack the beer into clean bottles when the gravity reaches 1.015 to 1.012.
10. To each bottle, add 1 teaspoon of corn sugar.

YIELD: 5 GALLONS

Sanitize for Success

Whenever you brew or bottle pumpkin beer or wine, sanitize all fermenters, carboys, stirring spoons, bottles, and other equipment with chlorine bleach, mixed ¼ cup to the gallon of warm water (30 ml/L). Set sanitized equipment aside for 20 minutes to let the bleach do its work, then rinse well before using.

Pumpkin Wine

An old pioneer song mentions early American wine made from an odd combination: "For we can make liquor to sweeten our lips of pumpkins and parsnips and walnut tree chips." Well, let me assure you that parsnips and tree chips aren't needed to make a perfectly nice pumpkin wine.

In the early days, pumpkin liquor was brewed right in the shell. Anne Copeland MacCallum, student of anthropology and self-published author of *Pumpkin, Pumpkin!* (now out of print), devised this modern version: Place a large pumpkin in a glass pan to control leaks. Cut off the top and remove the seeds and membranes. In the pumpkin's cavity combine 1 cup of brown sugar, two large boxes of chopped raisins, two packets of dried yeast, and the juice of two lemons. Allow the mixture to work until the pumpkin's flesh dissolves, then strain through several layers of cheesecloth. Put the liquid into a gallon jug or other large container and set it aside until the yeast settles, then rack off the liquid, taking care not to disturb the sediment. After fermentation stops (the brew will no longer bubble), pour your "wine" into bottles and cork them. You should have about 2½ quarts. Refrigerate and serve chilled.

Making pumpkin wine in a fermenter is much the same as brewing beer, with two differences.

- Wine can be more easily made in small batches. By making small batches, you can use an inexpensive 5-gallon, food-grade bucket as your fermenter and one or more 1-gallon jugs in place of a large, expensive carboy.
- Wine is more sensitive than beer to spoilage. Spoilage is easy to prevent, however, with meticulous cleanliness.

Some wine recipes call for cooked pumpkin, some call for raw pumpkin. Baking the pumpkin meat, or boiling it in some of the water you'll use for fermenting, sterilizes the flesh and releases its sugars and starches. Raw pumpkin, on the other hand, will give you a clearer wine.

Pumpkin Happy Wine

Emilio Rodrigues Vazquez uses cooked pumpkin in his wine, which he considers "smooth and delicate for special occasions. The more pumpkin you use, the heavier bodied will be your wine." This is an adaptation of the recipe Emilio contributed to Pumpkin Happy, *a hand-printed, stapled recipe booklet used as a fund-raiser for the floating environmental classroom, the Hudson River sloop* Clearwater. *Each October, the* Clearwater *embarks on an annual 2-week Pumpkin Sail, delivering its colorful autumn cargo to communities along the Hudson River.*

15–25 pounds raw pumpkin, grated

4½ gallons water
sugar or honey (For a dry wine: 7 lbs. For a normal wine: 10 lbs. For a sweet wine: 12 lbs.)

juice from 3 large lemons
1 packet wine yeast

1. Boil the grated pumpkin in the water for 20 minutes. Cool and strain into a fermenter through several layers of cheesecloth.
2. Add the sugar or honey in your desired quantities. Stir until it dissolves. Add the lemon juice.
3. Cool to 70°F (21°C). Add the wine yeast.
4. After fermentation stops, rack the wine into a carboy and set aside until the sediment settles to the bottom and the wine clears — about 3 months.
5. Siphon the wine into sterilized wine bottles, taking care not to stir up the sediment. You'll get a perfectly smooth drink if you leave behind a few inches of wine above the sediment. Cork the bottles and keep them upright. Store in a cool, dark closet or a cellar for *at least* 8 months.

YIELD: 5 GALLONS

Dry Pumpkin Wine

While he was co-owner of the Wine Works (a home beer- and wine-making supplier) in Denver, Colorado, Raymond Massaccesi wrote and published the Winemaker's Recipe Handbook, *containing simple recipes calling for everyday items such as pumpkins. Raymond suggests that pumpkin wine tastes best if you let it age for at least a year. If you wish to drink this wine young, or if you prefer sweet wine, stabilize and sweeten the wine at bottling time, as indicated in the recipe. To make more than 1 gallon at a time, proportionately increase all ingredients except the yeast (1 packet of yeast is enough to make 5 gallons of wine). To make a smoother wine, I've modified Raymond's recipe by adding a box of raisins along with the pumpkin meat. Acid blend, tannin, nutrient, and campden tablets are all available at home wine-making supply shops.*

5 pounds pumpkin, cleaned, peeled, and ground or mashed	1 teaspoon yeast nutrient
1 box raisins, chopped	¼ teaspoon tannin
9 pints boiling water	1 campden tablet
6⅓ cups sugar	1 package wine yeast
1 tablespoon acid blend	**Sweetener (optional)**
	½ teaspoon stabilizer
	½ cup sugar

1. Add the raisins to the pumpkin. Stir in the boiling water, sugar, acid blend, yeast nutrient, tannin, and campden tablet. Cover and set aside for 24 hours.
2. Add the wine yeast. Stir daily.
3. In 3 to 5 days, at a gravity of 1.040, strain the juice into a carboy.
4. Rack again in about 3 weeks, when the hydrometer reading reaches 1.000.
5. Rack again in 2 months, and again in 2 months, as necessary to clear.
6. *For sweet wine:* If you wish, combine a little wine with the stabilizer and sugar. Stir into the rest of the wine before bottling.
7. Siphon the wine into sanitized bottles.

YIELD: 1 GALLON

Pumpkin Vinegar

To make pumpkin vinegar, start as you would for wine, but let the brew come into contact with lots of air while it ages — instead of using an air lock, which allows gases to escape but not enter, loosely cover the fermenter with a clean towel.

Preserving Pumpkins

Prolific pumpkin vines mature all at once, offering a heap of ripe pumpkins to deal with. Most years here in hot, dry Tennessee, my pumpkins are ready to harvest by mid- to late August, when the weather is still too warm to store them for any length of time. I'm therefore sent into a frenzy of trying to preserve them all by canning, drying, and freezing. When we have the rare cool, damp summer and our pumpkins ripen later in the season, we set a few aside in the pantry for use throughout the fall.

Storing

I like to store whole pumpkins because they give me something "fresh" to serve when the gardening season is over. Late-maturing and hard-shelled varieties store best. Under the conditions we can provide, pepos of the Sugar variety won't keep as well as maximas. In our barn, spread out on hay bales so they don't touch, maximas last into April, while pepos tend to soften within a month or two. 'Jack-Be-Little' and related miniatures, on the other hand, keep well for eight months or more.

If you're fond of a particular variety, even if it's not rated high for storage, try growing and storing a sample to see how it holds up for you. Due to variations in climate, soil, and rainfall, cultivars perform differently in different areas. When you grow pumpkins for storage, go easy on the fertilizer — you want fruit that's firm and solid, not soft and mushy.

Store only pumpkins with 2-inch (5 cm) stems, and skin so tough you can't punch through it with your fingernail. Pumpkins with broken-off stems, and immature fruits with soft shells, won't store well. Immediately use (eat, can, dry, or freeze) any pumpkin with broken skin — it won't keep long. Take care not to drop or otherwise bruise a pumpkin, which hastens rot. And never carry a pumpkin by its stem; if the stem breaks off, the wound will soon rot.

Sound pumpkins keep well at a higher temperature and lower humidity than most produce, with the exceptions of other winter squash and sweet potatoes. Any sound whole pumpkin should keep for a month or more at room temperature and for up to four months in the refrigerator. It may keep for six months or more if stored, not touching, where the temperature remains close to 50°F (10°C) and the air is dry, or at around 55 percent relative humidity.

At temperatures lower than 50°F (10°C), the pumpkin's cell wall rapidly weakens, and the fruit collapses. At temperatures above 70°F (21°C), seeds sprout inside the pumpkin and the flesh turns mealy or stringy. Also, humidity is as important as temperature. If the humidity is too low, moisture evaporates and the pumpkin shrivels up. At high humidity, mold sets in.

Pumpkins will keep for several months if stored, not touching, where the temperature is around 55°F (10°C) and the relative humidity is 55 percent.

An inexpensive thermometer/hygrometer will help you find or create the ideal storage spot, which might be an unheated attic or dry basement. Store pumpkins on hay bales or slatted shelves, never on solid shelves or a cement floor, where the air flow is poor. Since pumpkins need good air circulation, store them in a single layer with space between, not in heaps.

Check your pumpkins occasionally and wipe off surface mold with a dry cloth. Remove pumpkins that feel soft at the stem or blossom end (indicating they won't last much longer) or have other soft spots (indicating that rot has already set in).

Curing

Curing a pumpkin before storing it hardens its shell and reduces its water content, thus lengthening the time it may be stored. Cure pumpkins by laying them out, whole and with stems intact, in a warm (70–80°F, 21–27°C) place. You can leave them in the field in the sun, but take care to cover them if rain or frost threatens. Pumpkins that have been bitten by frost won't keep.

When the weather is sunny and cool, curing in the field takes no more than a day. If conditions are damp, though, curing may take two to three days. Curing indoors takes three to five days. During curing, the skin will toughen and minor surface cuts will heal over. The warm temperature sweetens the flesh by accelerating the conversion of starches into sugar.

After the pumpkins have been cured, wipe their shells with a damp cloth dipped in a solution of 1 part chlorine bleach to 10 parts water. Wiping pumpkins is especially important if the ground is damp at harvest time. The chlorine bleach solution will minimize rotting by reducing bacteria and fungi on the shell. Since rot most often starts at the stem end, dip the stem up to its attachment point in the bleach solution and carefully blot off the excess.

Freezing

If you don't have an ideal place to store whole pumpkins, freeze the flesh either cooked or raw.

To freeze raw pumpkin, cut the seeded and peeled flesh into 1-inch (2.5 cm) cubes, spread them on baking sheets, and pop them into the freezer. When the cubes are frozen, pack them into airtight containers or plastic bags designed for freezer storage. Freezing raw pumpkin slows deterioration due to enzyme action, but doesn't stop it, so use the pumpkin fairly soon and don't expect it to be as firm as fresh pumpkin.

To freeze cooked pumpkin, first make a puree and let it cool. Pack the puree into airtight containers, leaving 1 inch (2.5 cm) of space at the top for expansion, or seal it in heat-sealed plastic bags. Pack just enough in each container for one recipe, and note the intended recipe on the label. A painless way to stock up on frozen purees to bake or steam a whole pumpkin when you prepare a meal, then freeze the unused portion. In a dedicated freezer, cooked puree will keep for up to a year.

Canning

Pumpkin is a low-acid food and therefore must be sealed under pressure to be safely canned. Can it diced, with or without salt, sugar, or spices.

To can it diced, place the cubes in a pot, cover them with water, and bring to a boil. Then transfer the cubes to hot, clean canning jars, leaving ½ inch (1 cm) of headspace. Fill the jars with hot cooking liquid, again leaving ½ inch (1 cm) of headspace. If you wish, add ½ teaspoon of salt per pint, 1 teaspoon per quart.

Alternatively, drain the hot pumpkin and can it in a hot syrup made by boiling for five minutes, 6 cups of water and 3 cups of sugar per seven 1-pint jars to be canned; if you wish, spice the syrup with six whole cloves or a crushed cinnamon stick. To avoid discoloring your pumpkin, strain out the spices before pouring the syrup over the hot cubes in the jars, again leaving ½ inch (1 cm) of headspace.

Following the manufacturer's directions for your pressure canner, process pumpkin at 11 pounds of pressure for:

- 55 minutes, for pints
- 90 minutes, for quarts

Drying

Dry pumpkins as soon after the harvest as possible. The old-time drying method was to slice whole pumpkins into thin rings, peel the rings, remove the seeds and stringy pulp from the centers, and hang the rings from a broom handle or other stick propped between rafters in the ceiling or attic.

Pumpkin may also be air-dried on a screen covered with cheesecloth. Clean and peel the flesh and slice it into strips ¼ inch (6 mm) thick. Spread the strips so they don't touch and cover them lightly with cheesecloth to keep off insects. Dry the strips in a warm place out of direct sunlight, turning them

Dried pumpkin has more nutrients and lasts longer than canned or frozen pumpkin.

twice daily. They should be fully dry in 6 to 10 days.

Pumpkin that has been air-dried should be pasteurized before storage to eliminate any possibility of insect eggs or larvae. Spread the dried chips loosely on baking trays and heat them in a 175°F (80°C) oven for 10 minutes. Let the chips just cool and immediately seal them in airtight containers.

If you have an oven that can be warmed to 140°F (60°C) or less, you may use it to dry pumpkin, too. The pilot light of a gas oven provides enough heat. With the door propped open, pumpkin slices should dry in four to six hours.

The surest way to dry pumpkin, though, is in a food dehydrator, operated according to the manufacturer's directions. Drying preserves more nutrients than either canning or freezing, and properly dried foods last almost indefinitely. I love to experiment with different ideas in my "Big One" dehydrator. Recently I covered pumpkin slices with sugar, as if I were going to make Hollis's Pumpkin Chips (see page 164), and the next morning I drained the slices and put them in the dryer. Every time I checked to test for doneness, I ate one (well, okay, two or three), and by the time those delicious chips should have been dry and ready for storage, they were all gone.

Drying takes 12 to 18 hours, depending on the thickness of the chips. Fully dried chips are either tough and leathery or light and brittle, depending on how thick you slice them to begin with. I find that slices I cut with a paring knife turn out chewy, while those I prepare in my Cuisinart slicer dry as crisp as potato chips.

Pumpkin flesh, like that of other produce, contains enzymes that cause deterioration, even after it has been dried. Most drying directions tell you to kill enzymes by blanching or steaming pumpkin slices before you dry them, but many pumpkin varieties fall apart as soon as the slices are heated through, giving you mush instead of chips.

Since enzymes require moisture, you can slow their action by making sure your pumpkin is thoroughly dry and by storing it in airtight containers where it won't be exposed to humidity. Heat-sealed plastic bags are ideal; canning jars with proper lids and rings also work well. Store containers in a cool, dry place. For long-term storage, slow enzyme action even further by putting containers in the refrigerator or freezer.

Pumpkin Flour

Native Americans showed the Pilgrims how to dry pumpkin and grind it into meal for year-round use. Corn bread made with pumpkin is still popular in some areas of the New England. Any recipe will gain food value, flavor, and color if you substitute pumpkin meal for a small part of the flour — say, ¼ to ½ cup.

I've seen instructions for grinding pumpkin flour from dried puree, but my attempts have ended in a gummy mess. Instead, I grind dried raw slices. In my Vitamix they become flour in less than a minute. Any blender or food processor should readily grind a coarse meal or a fine flour. I find that thin slices (sliced in a food processor) readily grind into flour, while thick slices tend to grind into a coarser meal. Either way, take care not to inhale the powder that billows up when you transfer the flour into an airtight container for storage.

Instant Pumpkin Pie Mix

Add 1½ teaspoons of pumpkin pie spice per cup of pumpkin powder. To reconstitute plain or spiced powder, combine with an equal amount of hot water and set aside for 30 minutes. For each cup of desired puree, reconstitute ¾ cup of powder; 1 cup of dried powder plus 1 cup of water will give you 1¼ cups of reconstituted pumpkin.

Pumpkin Leather

Pumpkin leather makes a tasty, healthful, chewy snack that's handy to carry in your purse or pocket, and is perfect for tucking into your back-pack as an energy food. Made with finely grated lemon rind, this leather has a pleasant fruity flavor but is best eaten within a day or two. If, instead, you add 1 teaspoon pumpkin pie spice (or the spices suggested below), your leather will take on a traditional pumpkin pie flavor that improves with age.

4 cups pumpkin puree
½ cup sugar
½ teaspoon lemon rind *or*
 ½ teaspoon cinnamon

¼ teaspoon nutmeg
¼ teaspoon cloves
 cornstarch

1. Combine all ingredients. Spread evenly on trays designed for making fruit leather, or on regular drying trays covered with plastic wrap.
2. When the leather is dry enough to peel from the tray, dust it lightly with cornstarch, roll it into a tube shape (or tear or cut it into serving-sized portions), and tightly wrap it in plastic. Store in a cool, dry place.

YIELD: 2 FRUIT ROLLS

Pumpkin Seeds

Before Columbus came to the Americas, the citizens of Mexico and Peru grew pumpkins just for their seeds. When the crop matured, they extracted the seeds and threw away the meat. As strange as this practice may sound today, the fact is that most of a pumpkin's nutritional value is in its seeds.

Known in the Southwest as pepitas, pumpkin seeds are a good source of fiber and are full of vitamin E, the B vitamins, iron, protein, and unsaturated fat. Hull-less varieties are higher in protein (nearly 40

hulled seed

hull-less seed

percent, compared to about 30 percent in hulled varieties) and highly unsaturated oil (40–45 percent compared to about 35 percent).

Naked seed varieties also have the clear advantage of not needing to be cracked. Just halve or quarter ripe pumpkins, scoop out the seeds, and rinse them in cold water — they'll separate from the fibrous pulp fairly easily. Dry the cleaned seeds on a piece of cheesecloth, a nonterry towel, or a food-safe screen at room temperature or slightly higher. A fan will help hasten drying, especially if the air is humid. Seeds are fully dry when they feel hard.

Seeds with hulls may be cleaned and dried the same way as hull-less seeds. Some pumpkin seed enthusiasts enjoy cracking hulled seeds between their teeth as a way to ease tension. Alternatively, here's Jan Vala's easy dehulling method: Break up the seeds with a rolling pin, hammer, or food chopper. Drop the broken seeds into a large container of water. Stir vigorously to ensure that all kernels come into contact with the water. The kernels will sink to the bottom while the shells float. Skim off the shells and throw them in the compost pile. Drain and dry the hulled kernels.

Due to their high oil content, which encourages rancidity, store pumpkin seeds as you would other fresh nuts — in airtight containers in the refrigerator or freezer. Add them to cereals, use them in place of nuts in baked goods, or enjoy them raw or toasted as a snack.

Toasting Seeds

Toasting pumpkin seeds is popular because it lets you enhance the flavor by adding salt and/or spices, and it crisps the hulls to make them easier to crack. But toasting also reduces the food value of pumpkin seeds and shortens their shelf life. While raw seeds will keep for several months or even years at room temperature or cooler, toasted seeds turn rancid in just a few months outside the refrigerator. Even if you prefer your seeds toasted, store them raw and toast them when you're ready to serve them. Our family much prefers the nutlike flavor of fresh seeds to what we consider to be a rancid taste even in freshly toasted seeds.

To toast or not to toast is a matter of personal taste, though, so here are several toasting methods for you to try. Serve the seeds while they're warm, or cool and refrigerate them in airtight containers.

Oven-toasted. Spread dried hulled seeds on a lightly oiled baking sheet. Sprinkle them with a little salt, if desired, and bake them at 250°F (120°C) for 40 minutes, or until the seeds are crisp and lightly browned. Shake or stir the seeds every 10 or 15 minutes so they won't burn.

Although pumpkin seeds are already high in oil, some people like to oil or butter them for toasting. In a bowl, add 1 tablespoon of vegetable oil or melted butter per cup of seeds and toss until the seeds are well coated.

If you wish to season your seeds, sprinkle them on the toasting trays with curry, garlic powder, onion powder, and/or dried herbs. For a zippy hot and spicy taste, sprinkle the seeds with Cajun spices or chili powder, cumin, and a dash of cayenne. For a delicate smoky flavor, lightly sprinkle them with smoked salt along with a little garlic powder and onion powder.

Boiled. In true southern fashion, some gourmets like to boil pumpkin seeds in brine before toasting them. Just how much salt to use, and how long to boil the seeds, is again a matter of taste. A good start is 1 teaspoon of salt and 1 cup of water per cup of seeds, simmered for at least 10 minutes. Alternatively, let the seeds soak in the brine overnight. Drain the seeds, pat dry, and toast as usual.

Pan-roasted. When you need hot pumpkin seeds in a hurry, roasting them in a skillet is faster than toasting them in the oven. Warm the skillet on low heat, add a little oil or butter, stir in the seeds, and sprinkle them with salt (and spices, if you wish). Stirring occasionally, fry the seeds until they swell and make popping sounds, which may take anywhere from 5 to 15 minutes, depending on the amount of seeds and how even your heat is.

Microwaved. Brent Loy, father of the naked-seeded 'Snackjack', suggests roasting seeds in the microwave. First soak them for two to three hours in a 7.5 percent brine solution, made by mixing 5 teaspoons of table salt per pint of water (5 ml salt/100 ml water). Then air-dry them so they'll puff up nicely during roasting. Place the seeds on a shallow microwave tray, cover the tray with plastic wrap, and microwave on high continuously (do not stop and start the oven) for three and a half minutes.

Pumpkin Seed Oil

If you have a bumper crop of pumpkin seeds, you might try extracting the oil. Naked seed pumpkins have long been grown in eastern Europe as an alternative to two other popular sources of cooking oil — canola and olives. Naked seed varieties contain more oil than hulled varieties.

Grind the seeds in a blender and set the meal aside until the oil rises to the top. If you want to use the oil in salad dressing, just pour it off. If you plan to use it in a skillet, strain it through a coffee filter to minimize burning. Use the remaining meal to thicken soups, stews, and sauces.

Sprouted Seeds

If you like alfalfa and mung bean sprouts, why not sprout some pumpkin seeds for a different flavor? Sprout only fresh seeds. Rinse the seeds and place 1 cup in a quart jar. Fill the jar with lukewarm water and cover it with cheesecloth or a sprouting screen. Let the seeds soak for 10 hours or overnight, then drain off the water.

Keep the jar in darkened, warm place, rinsing the seeds morning and evening. After four days, place the jar in the sunlight and continue rinsing until the sprouts are 1 inch (2.5 cm) long. If you're sprouting naked seeds, just rinse them and add them to salads or stir-fries. If you're sprouting a hulled variety, you'll have to pop the loosened hull from each sprout.

Nutritional Values

	Cooked Pumpkin, Fresh	Cooked Pumpkin, Commercially Canned	Pumpkin Seeds
Amount	I cup	I cup	I ounce
Weight	245 g	245 g	28.35 g
Water	94%	90%	7%
Calories	50	85	155
Protein	2 g	3 g	7 g
Total fat	0 g	I g	13 g
Saturated fat	0.1 g	0.4 g	2.5 g
Monounsaturated fat	0 g	0.1 g	4 g
Polyunsaturated fat	0 g	0 g	5.9 g
Cholesterol	0 g	0 g	0 g
Carbohydrates	12 g	20 g	5 g
Calcium	37 mg	64 mg	12 mg
Phosphorus	74 mg	86 mg	333 mg
Iron	1.4 mg	3.4 mg	4.2 mg
Potassium	564 mg	505 mg	229 mg
Sodium	2 mg	12 mg	5 mg
Vitamin A	2,650 IU	54,040 IU	110 IU
Vitamin E (retinol equivalents)	265	5,404	11
Thiamin	0.08 mg	0.06 mg	0.06 mg
Riboflavin	0.19 mg	0.13 mg	0.09 mg
Niacin	I mg	0.9 mg	0.5 mg
Ascorbic acid	12 mg	10 mg	0 mg

Source: "Nutritional Value of Foods," University of Tennessee Cooperative Extension Service

Appendix

Recommended Reading

Cookbooks

The New Pumpkin Book (1981) by Mary Bettencourt and Terry Pimsleur, Half Moon Bay Art & Pumpkin Festival, P.O. Box 274, Half Moon Bay, CA 94019. *68-page stapled booklet*

In Praise of Pumpkins (1990) by Mary Joan Barrett, History Unlimited, Box 171, Fineview, NY 13640, 613-923-2331. *104-page spiral-bound recipe book*

Pumpkin Happy (1976) by the Hudson River sloop *Clearwater,* 112 Market Street, Poughkeepsie, NY 12601, 914-454-7673, fax 914-454-7953. *Stapled recipe booklet used as an environmental fund-raiser*

Pumpkin Patch Recipes (1984) by Lin Ayers, The Pumpkin Patch, Faulkner Farm, 14292 Telegraph Road, Santa Paula, CA 93060. *Ring-bound bundle of recipe cards*

Vala's Pumpkin Patch Fall Fun Cookbook (1994), by Jan Vala, Vala's Pumpkin Patch, 12102 South 180th, Gretna, NE 68028, 402-332-4200. *180-page spiral-bound recipe book*

Children's and Crafts Books

In a Pumpkin Shell (1992) by Jennifer Storey Gillis, Storey Communications, Schoolhouse Road, Pownal, VT 05261, toll-free 800-441-5700. *More than 20 pumpkin projects, from starting a patch to carving jack-o'-lanterns and making pumpkin snacks*

The Pumpkin Book (1983) by Susan Olson Higgins, Pumpkin Press, P.O. Box 139, Shasta, CA 96087, 916-244-6251. *Parent-teacher Halloween projects sourcebook, including tips on growing, painting, and cooking*

Carving Jack-o'-Lanterns (1988) by Sam Gendusa, Annedawn Publishing, P.O. Box 247, Norton, MA 02766, 508-222-9069. *A sculptor's guide to carving giant pumpkins into formidable faces; excellent resource for schoolteachers and art instructors, as well as pumpkin carvers in general*

The Natural Soap Book by Susan Miller Cavitch, Storey Communications, Schoolhouse Road, Pownal, VT 05261, toll-free 800-441-5700.

Soap Recipes: Seventy Tried & True Ways to Make Modern Soap with Herbs, Beeswax & Vegetable Oils by Elaine C. White, Valley Hills Press

You Can Carve Fantastic Jack-o'-Lanterns (1989) by Rhonda J. Hart, Storey Communications, Schoolhouse Road, Pownal, VT 05261, toll-free 800-441-5700. *A beginner's pattern and instruction book*

Gardening Books

A Colour Atlas of Cucurbita Diseases (1994) by D. Blancard, John Wiley & Sons. *299 pages of technical information and color photographs of disease- and pest-infested vines*

Garden Seed Inventory by Ken Whealy, Seed Saver Publications, 3076 North Winn Rd., Decorah, IA 52101. *Annually updated inventory of seed catalogs listing open-pollinated varieties available in the United States and Canada.*

How to Grow Up to a 1,000-Pound Pumpkin (1992) by George Salovich, Howard Dill Enterprises, 400 College Road, RR 1, Windsor, NS B0N 2T0, Canada, 902-798-2728, fax 902-798-0842. *28-page stapled booklet containing history, growing tips, and recipes*

How to Grow World-Class Giant Pumpkins (1993) by Don Langevin, Annedawn Publishing, P.O. Box 247, Norton, MA 02766, 508-222-9069. *Complete guide to growing maximas for competition*

The New Seed-Starter's Handbook (1988) by Nancy Bubel, Rodale Press, 33 East Minor Street, Emmaus, PA 18098. *Step-by-step guide to starting plants from seed*

The Pumpkin King — Howard Dill & the Atlantic Giant (1992) by Al Kingsbury, A Way with Words, 83 Apple Tree Lane, Kentville NS B4N 5C1, Canada. *Paperback biography of the man who developed the Dill's Atlantic Giant*

Saving Seeds (1990) by Marc Rogers, Storey Communications, Schoolhouse Road, Pownal, VT 05261, toll-free 800-441-5700. *Gardener's guide to growing and storing garden seeds*

Seed to Seed (1991) by Suzanne Ashworth, Seed Saver Publications, 3076 North Winn Rd., Decorah, IA 52101. *Seed pollination and saving techniques and extensive lists of varieties within each pumpkin species*

Hand-outs

"Commercial Vegetable Production" by the Cooperative Extension Service, University of Maryland, P.O. Box 169, Queenstown, MD 21658, 410-827-8056, fax 410-827-9039. *Annually updated information on chemical control of pumpkin diseases and plant pests*

"Growing Giant Pumpkins" (1995) by Wayne Hackney, 227 Carmen Hill #2, New Milford, CT 06776. *Inexpensive 28-page booklet packed with beginner's information*

"A Small-Scale Agriculture Alternative: Pumpkins" by the USDA-OSSA, Ag Box 2244, Washington, DC 20250-2244, 202-401-1805, fax 202-401-1804. *Two-page overview of commercial growing*

"Suppliers of Beneficial Organisms in North America" by the California Environmental Protection Agency, EM&PM Division, 1020 N Street, Sacramento, CA 95814, 916-324-4100. *List of sources of beneficial predators*

"Pumpkin Cost of Production" by the Rutgers Cooperative Extension Service of Burlington County, 49 Rancocas Road, Mount Holly, NJ 08060, 609-265-5050, fax 609-265-5613. *Handout for commercial growers*

Organizations

Atlantic Pumpkin Growers' Association, P.O. Box 901, Windsor, NS B0N 2T0, Canada, 902-798-2728, fax 902-798-0842. *Competitive growers of giant pumpkins*

The Cucurbit Network, P.O. Box 560483, Miami, FL 33256. *Biennial newsletter related to cucurbit education and research*

Great Pumpkin Commonwealth, c/o Hugh Wiberg, 445 Middlesex Avenue, Wilmington, MA 01887, 508-658-5852. *Coalition of official giant-pumpkin weigh-off sites throughout the United States and Canada*

International Pumpkin Association, Inc., Terry Pimsleur, President, 2155 Union Street, San Francisco, CA 94123, 415-346-4446. *Sponsors annual giant-pumpkin weigh-off*

New England Pumpkin Growers Association, c/o Hugh Wiberg, 445 Middlesex Avenue, Wilmington, MA 01887, 508-658-5852. *Informative quarterly newsletter for competitive growers of giant pumpkins*

The World Pumpkin Confederation, Ray Waterman, President, 14050 Gowanda State Road, Collins, NY 14034, 716-532-5995. *Sponsors a giant-pumpkin weigh-off and distributes seeds from prizewinners*

Meetings

Annual Pumpkin Grower's Meeting, c/o Raymond J. Samulis, County Agricultural Agent, Rutgers Cooperative Extension Service of Burlington County, 49 Rancocas Road, Mount Holly, NJ 08060, 609-265-5050, fax 609-265-5613

Annual Grower's Information Meeting, c/o Lisa Norcross, 515 Goderich Street, Port Elgin, ON N0H 2C4, Canada, 519-389-3714 or 800-387-3456

Carving Supplies

Concept Marketing, P.O. Box 1705, Santa Rosa, CA 94502, 707-545-4171. *Safety candleholders and carving saws; deluxe carving kit includes tools, pattern book for children*

Pumpkin Masters, Box 61456, Denver, CO 80206, 303-722-4442, fax 303-871-9477. *Carving kits include tools, step-by-step instructions, new patterns every two years*

Carving Contests

Pumpkin Masters, Box 61456, Denver, CO 80206, 303-722-4442, fax 303-871-9477. *Carving contest*

The Seed Corps, P.O. Box 1705, Santa Rosa, CA 95402, 707-545-4171, fax 707-575-3707. *Jack-o'-lantern photo contest*

Pumpkin Seed Sources

For an updated listing of varieties and sources consult:

Garden Seed Inventory
Seed Savers Exchange
3076 North Winn Rd.
Decorah, IA 52101

As Grown Seed Company
7000 Portage Road
Kalamazoo, MI 49001
616-323-4000

Berlin Seeds
5371 County Road 77
Millersburg, OH 44654
216-893-2811

W. Altee Burpee & Company
300 Park Avenue
Warminster, PA 18974-0001
215-674-4900
800-333-5808

Burrell Seed Company
P.O. Box 150
Rocky Ford, CO 81067
719-254-3318

Comstock, Ferre & Company
236 Main Street
Wethersfield, CT 06109
203-529-3319

William Dam Seeds
279 Highway #8
West Flamboro, ON
Canada L9H 6M1

Howard Dill Enterprises
400 College Road, RR 1
Windsor, NS B0N 2T0
Canada
902-798-2728
Fax: 902-798-0842

Farmer Seed and Nursery
Faribault, MN 55021
507-334-1623

**Henry Field's Seed &
Nursery**
415 North Burnett
Shenandoah, IA 51602
605-665-4491

Fisher's Garden Store
P.O. Box 236
Belgrade, MT 59714
406-388-6052
Seeds for northern gardens

Gleckler's Seedmen
Metamora, OH 43540
(no phone)
*Unusual and early American
varieties*

J. L. Hudson, Seedman
Star Route 2, Box 337
La Honda, CA 94020
(no phone)
Please send $1 for catalog

Le Jardin du Gourmet
P.O. Box 75
St. Johnsbury Center, VT 05863

Johnny's Selected Seeds
Foss Hill Road
Albion, ME 04910
207-437-9294

McFayden Seeds, Ltd.
P.O. Box 1060
Brandon, MB R74 6E1
Canada

Nichols Garden Nursery
1190 North Pacific Highway
Albany, OR 97321
503-928-9280
Fax: 503-967-8406

Ontario Seed Co., Ltd.
330 Phillip Street
P.O. Box 144
Waterloo, ON N2J 3Z9
Canada

Park Seed Company
Cokesbury Road
Greenwood, SC 29647-0001
803-223-7333
Fax: 803-941-4206

Pinetree Garden Seeds
RR 1, Box 397
New Gloucester, ME 04260

P. L. Rohrer & Bro., Inc.
P.O. Box 250
Smoketown, Lancaster, PA 17576
717-299-2571
Lots of varieties

Vesey's Seeds
York
Prince Edward Island C0A 1P0
Canada

Rupp Seeds, Inc.
17919 County Road B
Wauseon, OH 43567
419-337-1841
The most varieties I've ever seen in one catalog

Sand Hill Preservation Center
1878 230th Street
Calamus, IA 52729
319-246-2299
Heirloom varieties

Seeds Blum
Idaho City Stage
Boise, Idaho 83706
208-336-8264
Heirloom varieties

Shepherd's Garden Seeds
30 Irene Street
Torrington, CT 06790
203-482-3638
Fax: 203-482-0532; or
408-335-6910
Fax: 408-335-2080

R. H. Shumway's
P.O. Box 1
Graniteville, SC 29829
803-663-9771

Southern Seeds
P.O. Box 2091
Melbourne, FL 32902
407-727-3662
Fax: 407-728-8493
Seminole pumpkin for hot climates

Stokes Seeds, Inc.
Box 548
Buffalo, NY 14240
416-688-4300

Stokes Seeds Ltd.
29 James Street, P.O. Box 10
St. Catharines, ON L2R 6R6
Canada

T&T Seeds Ltd.
111 Lombard Avenue
Winnepeg, MB R3C 3P6
Canada

Territorial Seed Company
P.O. Box 157
Cottage Grove, OR 97424
503-942-9547
Fax: 503-942-9881

Evergreen Y. H. Enterprises
P.O. Box 17538
Anaheim, CA 92817
Japanese pumpkins

**Vermont Bean Seed
Company**
Garden Lane
Fair Haven, VT 05743
802-273-3400
Fax: 802-663-9771

Willhite Seed Company
P.O. Box 23
Poolville, TX 76076
817-599-8656
Fax: 817-599-5843

Converting Recipe Measurements to Metric

In the recipes throughout this book, temperature conversions from Fahrenheit to Celsius have already been given, rounded to the nearest five degrees to provide practical, realistic oven settings.

In measuring most ingredients, whether liquid or dry, American cooks go by volume rather than by weight, using standardized teaspoons, tablespoons, and cups. Occasionally, liquids are measured in fluid ounces, and fruit and canned goods are measured in pounds and (avoirdupois) ounces. The following chart is offered to help overseas readers comprehend our quirky American system.

American	Metric
¼ teaspoon	1.25 ml
½ teaspoon	2.5 ml
1 teaspoon	5 ml
½ tablespoon (1½ teaspoon)	7.5 ml
1 tablespoon (3 teaspoons)	15 ml
⅛ cup (2 tablespoons)	30 ml
¼ cup (4 tablespoons)	60 ml
⅓ cup (5 tablespoons + 1 teaspoon)	80 ml
½ cup (8 tablespoons)	120 ml
1 cup (16 tablespoons)	240 ml
1 quart (4 cups)	950 ml
1 gallon (4 quarts)	3.8 L
1 fluid ounce (2 tablespoons)	30 ml
8 fluid ounces (1 cup)	240 ml
1 ounce	28.4 g
1 pound (16 ounces)	454 g
1 inch	2.5 cm

Index

Bold indicates chart material; Italics indicate illustrations

Other Storey Titles You Will Enjoy

Brewing Made Easy: From the First Batch to Creating Recipes, by Joe Fisher & Dennis Fisher. In ninety-six pages, Joe and Dennis Fisher have written the simplest brewing directions in modern history. A book for beginners and wannabes, the authors guide the reader through the very basics of recipe formulation all the way to creating new recipes, aided by step-by-step illustrations by graphic artist Randy Mosher. 96 pages. Paperback. ISBN 0-88266-941-9.

Garden Way's Joy of Gardening, by Dick Raymond. In this bestselling gardening "bible," Dick Raymond shares his proven methods for raised beds, wide rows, and other techniques for a bigger harvest with less work. 384 pages. Paperback. ISBN 0-88266-319-4.

Garden Way's Joy of Gardening Cookbook, by Janet Ballantyne. This is the classic book for anyone cooking with fresh vegetables. Organized by vegetable for ease of use, it includes more than 350 how-to-do-it and how-to-serve-it color photos to illustrate the text. 336 pages. Paperback. ISBN 0-88266-355-0.

The Herbal Body Book: A Natural Approach to Healthier Hair, Skin, and Nails, by Stephanie Tourles. This book explains how to transform common herbs, fruits, and grains into safe, economical, and natural personal care items. It contains more than 100 recipes to make facial scrubs, hair rinses, shampoos, soaps, cleansing lotions, moisturizers, lip balms, toothpaste, powders, insect repellants, and more. Each recipe also includes preparation time, yield, and storage and usage tips. 128 pages. Paperback. ISBN 0-882660-880-3.

In a Pumpkin Shell: Over 20 Pumpkin Projects for Kids, by Jennifer Storey Gillis. Lively, whimsical illustrations by Patti Delmonte are the perfect companion to over twenty fun pumpkin projects geared towards children ages four through ten. 64 pages. Paperback. ISBN 0-88266-771-8.

The Natural Soap Book: Making Herbal and Vegetable-Based Soaps, by Susan Miller Cavitch. Cavitch explores the goodness of soap, homemade without chemical additives and synthetic ingredients. Along with basic vegetable-based soap recipes, readers will find ideas on scenting, coloring, cutting, trimming, and wrapping soaps. The book also includes the history of soap through the ages, the effects of certain ingredients on the skin, a troubleshooting guide, and gift ideas. 144 pages. Paperback. ISBN 0-88266-888-9.

The New Zucchini Cookbook, by Nancy C. Ralston and Marynor Jordan. This book includes more than 190 delicious and healthy recipes. One entire chapter focuses on methods of preparing zucchini: baking, grilling, sauteing, stir-frying, stuffing, and tempura. 176 pages. Paperback. ISBN 0-88266-589-8.

You Can Carve Fantastic Jack-O-Lanterns, by Rhonda Massingham Hart. This book contains more than 60 large-size patterns of ghouls and spooks ready to be traced onto a pumpkin. Accessories and props are also suggested. 112 pages. Paperback. ISBN 0-88266-580-4.

These books and other Storey books are available at your bookstore, farm store, garden center, or directly from Storey Publishing, Schoolhouse Road, Pownal, Vermont 05261, or by calling 1-800-441-5700. www.storey.com